The Anxiety of Nonexistence

The Anxiety of Nonexistence

Márcio Faustino Santos

www.marciofaustino.com

ISBN: 9798683059743

www.marciofaustino.com

CONTENTS

STREET PORTRAITS AND NO VIOLENT COMMUNICATION

I remember 15 years ago when I used to see people everywhere talking about the democratization of information, of learning and of expression thanks to the internet, where anyone can share their knowledge and opinions. The free information accessible to all. It is ironic seeing fake news and conspiracy theories popularized nowadays.

When I was about 14 years old, in 1997, bullying and other sorts of insults were considered kind of normal, at least in my neighbourhood in Brazil. Often such kind of provocation wasn't taken seriously despite verbal aggressiveness. This provocative communication was somehow the standard nevertheless, meaning people verbally attacking and defending themselves with further attacks. It was in São Paulo, a city in which I believe to have an aggressive communication culture probably because of socioeconomic gaps, along, or as consequence, of prejudices; Prejudices often disguised as jokes.

On a weekend I met a friend who was arguing with a bunch of other guys a couple of years older than us. They were calling him stupid and laughing at him because he said Alberto Santos-Dumont was the inventor of wristwatch[1]. This was information I also believed to be true but back then I would never waste time and get angry trying to convince others about what I believed to be true, maybe because life seemed to be too stressful that I would rather avoid any more stress. So I called my friend inviting him to hang out somewhere else and, somehow, helping him to distance from the situation he was in. Still stupefied while we were walking away, he was explaining the other guys didn't want to believe in him. I replied to him suggesting to let it go. At that time I had not conceptualized it yet but I felt there were many people who were not curious and interested in knowing things but, instead, interested only in self-affirmation. *I feel I am right so you must be wrong.* Without any real argument in order to explain why they are right they rely on verbal violence, by offending and making the opponent angry in order to feel as the winner of the argument. Honestly, this kind of conversation and its violence is what I see being popularized the most in the internet.

Recently I have been wondering if we really can teach others. My thinking is that probably people only learn things if they want to (curiosity or duty) or if the situation is conducive to learning. If such thinking is somehow true the goal of teaching is not only to provide information but also help creating the situation that is propitious for learning, and this may be the reason why the internet is dominated by fake-news and conspiracy theory believers; A place where everyone can spread ideas of any kind in a moment of economic and, consequently, social distress.

When I began with street photography I was apprehensive about people's reactions. What would they think? What if they get angry? Then I thought if there are others doing it I can do it as well. It was in Ireland where I had the most friendly encountering with strangers ever but my first attempt to stop someone and ask if I could take a portrait of them was considered a shameful failure by me at the time. What my subject said that made me feel ashamed was a single simple word: "No". So I went home frustrated for not obtaining what I was expecting. I watched some videos about street photography and one hour later I was in the street trying again. This time I told myself to not expect anything. If people say "no" it is ok and there is nothing wrong about it. Actually, we are supposed to take risks in order to learn and grow, in order to see what is possible and what is not, and in order to lose ties from expectations that narrow our perception about things. With this twist of mind I endured a couple of other "no"s before hearing a "Sure". From that moment on I felt there was nothing to worry about.

With experience I have learned to improve my communication. Being more direct and specific, asking as a suggestion or as an offer and not as an expectation or demand. One of the main reasons for violent communication is the thinking that what others are asking is an order instead of a request. People hate to do things when they are demanded to and the natural reaction is to reject it. On the other hand we all like to feel useful and helpful. Antonio Damasio tells, in his book called **Looking for Spinoza,** that our brain produces serotonin, which gives us a well-being feeling, when we help or cooperate with others as a team. It is part of our empathy which makes us place ourselves in others' shoes, sensing people's emotion and feelings as our own.

Marshall Rosenberg, who wrote **No Violent Communication**, tells a story of an interview with a Nazi war criminal who was asked "Was it hard to send ten of thousand of people to death?", which he answered "No, it was easy. Easy because our language makes it easy". Then, he explained that his fellow officers had a name for this language: *Amtsprechen*, the bureaucratic language; A language that denies options, consequently it denies responsibility. It is interesting to know that there are many people who can not distinguish between rule, or law, and morality, which is the same as distinguishing can or can't from should and shouldn't. When we try to obtain some kind of alternative collaboration for a solution which would help makes all the parties happier, or less stressed, such kind of people are not able to do it, they start quoting what they believe to know about the law and their rights, meaning *I can do it (what the law says) so I will not do what you want me to do.* Basically, they view others' requests as demands and in return they react in a defensive way. They don't understand the saying *Just because you can do it, it doesn't mean you should do it (in consideration of others).*

In Ireland, after I got used to street photography, most people I had approached were happy to let me photograph them, which they saw as a request that they could help me with. In Germany, most of my attempts with street portraits has resulted in rejection. Some people even get angry with my approach and they can become verbally violent. I see it as a social phobia, worrying that I want do something bad with the photo I took of them, such as judge them or use the image for commercial purposes; worrying about what might happens with a photo someone took of them, where can it end up and who will be able to see it; worrying about my approach has a second intention such as selling things, demanding money or sexual intention when I am approaching women. In short, they have a lot of expectations which place them in the fear zone.

I think the coolest Germans are in Hamburg – although I have not been in most German regions yet. It was in Hamburg that I met Lucie Nechanická. We used to meet and wander in the streets to photograph it together. When she saw me approaching strangers and asking them if I could make a portrait of them she looked apprehensive, saying she would not feel comfortable doing it, which reminded me when I was attempting it for the first time in Dublin.

Even still doing it in Germany, I do not feel as confident and easy as I was in Ireland, reason why I approach people less often. But having Lucie on my side was different because she is a woman transmitting other women a sense of safety with my approach. People actually became more friendly thanks to her. It was most evident when I was waiting for Lucie in a train station and around the place there were people waiting to meet their friends as well. While waiting, I saw a woman with a cool outfit, nice hair and interesting tatoo on her leg, so I came to her asking if I could take a photograph of her. She looked at me with doubt and unsure but suddenly Lucie arrived saying "you don't waste time" to me. After my subject saw Lucie, and realized we knew each other, she readily accepted to be photographed.

Attempting street portraits in Hamburg is much easier than in other places I have been in Germany, but people still have some kind of fear about interaction with strangers. It is a different world than in Ireland where I could talk and photograph most people, especially women, without any tension and I think it reflects in the way people communicate, in their language, in their expectation and, consequently, in how they learn and perceive other kinds of experiences.

Unlike when I was a boy, I have recently engaged in useless arguments with people who didn't want to believe in what I was saying (in the internet), consequently I was annoyed and offended with their provocation – calling me stupid and names. Later on I was wondering why I was behaving like that. What changed? Did I forget my youth knowledge? And the only thing I could think about was my reality change, which has created different expectations and frustration; therefore changing my experiences and learning. I am now in a process of no violence redeem.

1. Some people say the world's first wristwatch was created by Abraham-Louis Breguet for Caroline Murat, Queen of Naples, in 1810. By the mid nineteenth century, most watchmakers produced a range of wristwatches, often marketed as bracelets, for women.

CREATION AND FRUSTRATION

As a newborn we don't know there existed a world before us, we don't know the things and people we see, hear and interact with were there before we came to the world, we don't even know the concept of *before*. When newborns cry as a reaction of the uncomfortable or painful feeling of hunger their mother offers milk from her breast while for newborns it is as if they have created the milk out of his cries. Not only that, it is as if they have created the breast, as if it is appearing from nowhere; For newborns, even their mothers are their own creation, as everything that is out there and comes in contact with them[1]. In **The Child, The Family And The Outside World** Donald Winnicott explains it is natural for newborns to feel as if everything comes from them. It is not a thinking, not a conceptualization in their heads (since they have none) but only a sensation.

If we feel people and things come from us, then, it is as if they are us. It is especially true in relation with newborns and mothers who experience the most frequent and intense touch, glance and care; who the newborn recognizes their mother's voice, the movements of her body and the heartbeat when in her womb.

The process of growing up is a phase of frustration, because it is when we face the harsh reality we can not have things as they would please us and whenever we want them. It is when we start to realize our mothers as independent individuals, when we realize that things don't disappear when we don't see, feel and hear them anymore but they go somewhere else, in another place and reality that exists independent from us and was there before us came to the world.

Winnicott explains that it is important for the child to express their frustration. The frustration expression happens in many ways; by associating people and things with good or bad personalities they learn from stories; by expressing and illustrating such associations in drawings and through playing – which Winnicott described as a serious thing for the child – because it is through playing children try to make sense of the world and express their feelings; by expressing the act of love or hate and even destruction when the frustration feels unbearable, such as kicking doors and throwing things on the floor in anger. When toddlers are repressed, forbidden or punished for being aggressive or destructive they express their frustration in dreams, often as a nightmare.

> "Remember that there is no better feeling in infancy or childhood than that which belongs to true spontaneous recovery from sadness and guilt feelings. This is so true that sometimes you will find your child beings naughty so as to feel guilty and cry, and then feel forgiven, so eager is he to recapture what he has experienced in true recovery from sadness" (p.67)

All expression, of any kind, is an act of creation and destruction of our wishes and frustration – even for grown ups. The act of building, shaping, drawing and interacting are acts of creation that often help us to deal with things in life that we can not have as we wished. Building, shaping, painting and drawing in an aggressive, freak or antic manner can be an expression of destruction. At the end what differs adults from toddlers other than becoming civilized? – Learning to repress and express our feelings of love (creation) and frustration (destruction) in a civilized way?

Depending on how we were allowed to overcome our unbearable frustrations is how we learn to deal with it in adult life. Not being able to overcome our natural frustration while growing up creates damaged adults who become little dictators, manipulative, aggressive, expressing their emotional pains by being mean with people, through aggressive identitarian expression (such as football team support or nationalism) or through political and ideological position as representation of good and evil to be fought and imposed as they wish. It is the wanting to create the world the way they wish and the frustration of not being able to that turns people nihilists.

Art helps us to deal with our feelings. It helps us to become civilized. It is the playing and the symbolic association we do to things, just as toddlers do, which deep inside is always a serious thing for helping us to make sense of this world. Every act and interaction is an expression; From the little help we offer to strangers, with mean comments some people make about others' appearances, also in art (especially in confusing art), all is a form of expression.

"I shall pretend he is conscious of what is going on, though he is not really. He is making a picture. What does he do? He knows the impulse to scribble and to make mess. That is not a picture. These primitive pleasures have to be kept fresh, but at the same time he wants to express ideas, and also to express them in such a way that they may possibly be understood. If he archives a picture he has found a series of controls that satisfies him. [...] Then he knows that the picture when it is finished must have balance – you know, the

tree on either side of the house – this is an expression
of the fairness which he needs and probably gets from
the parents. […] Within this system of accepted,
indeed self-imposed, controls he tries to express an
idea, and keep some of the freshness of feeling that
belonged to the idea when it was born. […] Yet your
children archive it quite naturally if you will give
them half a chance." (p.94)

Maybe because of its expressiveness representation people normally expect art to have a message, thus they try to interpret what pieces of art say or what they are about, turning art into an utilitarian object that needs to have an explanation in order to be accepted and recognized as *art*. Susan Sontag says, in her essay called **Against Interpretation**, that art is not about something; art is not supposed to have an utilitarian use for the public who appreciate and collect it. Art is a thing of its own. Its only use is to experience it. Sense it as we are supposed to sense the world around us – shapes, sounds, colours, texture, composition patterns and so on. The same happens when a child kicks a door because of frustration. It is not a message but a sole expression of frustration; Something to be experienced in order to overcome the frustration; A hope that out of the destruction a greater figure will establish order in their inner world experiencing confusion. Reason why adults should not ask toddlers why they are misbehaving; They don't know and, according to Winnicott, such question only creates more confusion and frustration in their heads which cause them to overthink, leading them to mental stress and depression.

We can create and recreate meanings according to our own individual or collective understanding and experiences. Meanings are important, they are the associative representation we use to make sense of the world. Consequently, we use meanings in our conceptual expression. But meaning and truth are not the same thing so art is not about the message it carries (the meaning we give to it) but about the experiencing of its expressiveness, as creation and destruction, as overcoming our deep painful and unbearable feelings that cause us to overthink, so we can quite our mind and experience the fulfilling calm stillness behind everything, after the fulfilling act.

1 "A thousand times the feeling has existed that what was wanted was created, and was found to be there. From this development a believe that the world can contain what is wanted and needed, with the result that the baby has hope that there is a live relationship between inner reality and external reality, between innate primary creativity and the world at large which is shared by all". (WINNICOTT, D.W. *The Child, The Family, and The Outside World*. Cambridge: Perseus Publishing, 1964 p.90)"

LOVE, FEAR, CHRISTIANITY AND CRISIS

Without Agape there is no Christianity. Those who speak about Christianity without Agape are not Christians but something else. Agape is the most pure Christian love. It is the love for God through people and the love for people through God, unconditionally. Through such love people become able to recognize themselves in others, so being able to love themselves in others, where they find God. Agape is, essentially, the ability to find God within one's self through empathy and, consequently, find God in others. This was at the heart of Jesus' message and it's less about religion than it is about psychology.

Neuroscientists and Psychoanalysts, such as Stuart Brown and Winnicott, discovered that there is a correlation between play and empathy. In short, the more time we spend interacting with people in a relaxed manner and for no reason at all (playing and art), specially during our brain development while we are growing up, the more we develop a sense of empathy, which is the ability to imagine oneself in others' situation (being able to recognize ourselves in others).

True empathy has no utilitarian meaning; the empathic person is not looking for any reward or gratification from their empathic act, other than the happiness that comes from treating others as they would wish to be treated themselves, as if they are acting towards themselves that they find in others' shoes. Jesus literally interpreted it as unconditional love, which in order to have people have to find God in themselves – the security against their own fears.

If we mistake Agape for Philia, which is the love for oneself only – and not for God – for utilitarian relations (also known as fraternal love), such Christianism is not the one that came from Jesus but from the Church as institution, that emerged inside the Roman's patriarch tradition and proto-capitalist culture.

The opposite of Philia, as well as Agape, is Phobia; the irrational fear of what one believes to be an imminent threat or danger. Those who have Phobia struggle finding God in themselves so they tend to feel on their own when dealing with their tragic fates. When one is unable to find God inside themselves they are not able to find God inside others (particularly those who they consider to be a threat), therefore they are not able to feel empathy – they tend to become cynical; Essentially, not being able to love God through people and love people through God.

It is also important not to mistake Agape for Storge, the instinctive love for your family and those considered as family. It is especially terrible if Agape is confused with Eros, the carnal or erotic love – a physical desire and the love for what feels beyond us.

Maybe because the Jewish spent so long time wandering in the desert without a land of their own, in the biblical time, they believed they were being punished by God. Jesus, who was a Jewish, came up with another interpretation about God; A God of love and not a God of fear. Jesus had a libertarian preach from both Jewish and Roman moral laws that became strong in their social crisis, so he ended up crucified by both. But Jesus wasn't alone in his view about conservative traditions because Greek tragedies also taught people about the dangers of rationalism (born with Socrates), its individualism and patriarchal traditions that attempt to control nature out of fear. Greek tragedies tell us that nature and its mysteries can not be controlled because it has its natural symbiosis which we can not fully understand, so we can not escape our fate that is part of such symbiosis – our tragedy. But Jesus had a positive love message, about how we can find comfort in each other despite our fates; Such love is literally God. Once Christianity is institutionalized under Roman economic, political and military brotherhood tradition (Philia) and rationalism – under wish was born the self-consciousness and, consequently, the responsibility of each one for their own fate – agape faded away and was mistaken with another kind of love; a materialist love.

Jesus' message has a lot in common with the oriental metaphysical religiosity. For this reason some people speculate that Jesus may have traveled to the Far-Eastern Orient where he might have learned the bases for his messages. I don't know about that. I prefer to believe that Jesus was just an average guy who had a metaphysical experience and interpreted such experience in the monotheist language of his religious tradition, as Alan Watts suggested. Especially considering Jesus wasn't the only one who, by intuition, could feel and understand something beyond common understanding during his time and culture. Think about Greek philosophers and mythologies, Taoist monks or even Spinoza and Einstein in more recent historical times. Many centuries later – or a few years later if considering modern thinkers – a lot of what they realized by intuition became accepted by rationalism and in many cases confirmed by empiricism.

If people have fear and they are not able to recognize such fear in themselves – especially because they want to be 'tough' or fit in a group for social standing – such fear turns into hate. In order to not hate oneself, for feeling weak or vulnerable, they tend to transfer such hate towards outside the self; towards others. Without realizing it hate becomes a cycle of self-victimization; a product of the fear which people find in themselves.

RULES ARE FOR REPRODUCTION, AND FOR PEOPLE WHO CAN NOT FEEL OR TRUST THEIR INNER VOICE [YET]

We need rules as a reference or start point when we are introduced to new activities, when we have not much from ourselves to put in a new work but practice, get inspired through copy and to fit in trying results with a predetermined expectation. We can get great pleasures from reproduction; from the empathic recognition from other creators; for its social integration feeling; or from the observation of transformation through tools manipulation. By doing so, we can develop our own feeling, a personal way to create and a voice to express.

I saw once a documentary about French soldiers returning home after the second World War; the war that had more dead and injured soldiers, perhaps because of the huge number of soldiers sent to fight. When survivor and fit-to-work soldiers returned home after the war, looking for their families and labour routines, that were occupied by women during the war, they found themselves lost as if they lacked identity and purpose. As soldiers those men got used to following orders, giving themselves to the battalion rhythm for its greater performance – the fellowship was their identity. Later on in society, working in their farms, shops and industries, they found themselves on their own with their individual decisions for their personal lives and activities, in their own rhythm. What was missing was their inner voices.

I can't help but see some similarities between these soldiers and the corporation-made teamwork culture, especially in the 80's and 90's when workers were encouraged to see businesses they worked for as part of their families; where one finds their purpose and identity through the job and culture provided within the business.

Behind it all there is the fixation, the focus which people become alienated. In **Willing Slaves of Capital** Frédéric Lordon says alienation is not loss but fixation. The more limited is your attention and experiences range (fixed), the more alienated you find yourself. Through alienation it is easier to drive the work and goals of a person or group of people to a determined direction – a direction determined by the aims of the leader but which the followers take as their own aim[1].

For Oswald Spengler, in **Prussianism and Socialism**, the Teutonic (Germanic) tribes have such principles as tradition; the military and hierarchical rules in their social culture, expecting people to give up their personal goals and interests in order to follow their social hierarchy determinism, looking forwards to the greater completion of their *nation* (society) as their own individual aim – instead of looking towards climbing the social hierarchy for individual achievement[2]. In situations like this workers can focus only on improving their ability to work and behave as expected from their social standing (like in the army), instead of the distraction of individual dreams that look for novelty and expect, eventually, to reach somewhere else. It is the type of alienation where people get attached to rules for their guidance and once deeply alienated they get lost, disorientated and messy when missing a leader to follow as their own goals and identity.

The opposite is the ability to listen to our own inner voice, our timing; to have a wide scope to observe and to react in accordance and spontaneously to each situation by following our guts, when rules are not what give us direction anymore but what make us feel limited – limiting our experiences, our observations, our experimentations, our self learning and our expression. When dealienation becomes necessary because rules funnel us to the alien aim that we take as our own.

Listening to our own inner voice is not the same as individualism and selfishness because when we are listening to our inner voice we are listening to others around us as well, sensing the world around us and trusting our feelings; our attention and expressions take others in consideration.

Rules are for reproduction, and for creators who can not feel or trust their inner voice [yet]. A true creative work is a work that has its own voice and rhythm. A sincere self expression and feeling.

1 LORDON, F. "Joyful Auto-Mobiles (Employees: How to Pull Their Legs)" in *Willing Slaves Of Capital: Spinoza and Marx on Desire*. London: Verso, 2014

2 SPENGLER, O. *Preussentum und Sozialismus*, 1920, Translated 1922 as Prussianism And Socialism by C.F.Atkinson.

ART, THINKING, REALITY AND THE CONTEMPLATIVE MIND

The comedian Jim Carrey said in an interview that, with his comedy, he has realized what all people want: to be free from concern. Despite the fact people usually don't take him seriously I don't think he said it casually. We tend to believe that through thinking we will find understanding of things, solutions to problems and knowledge but often we think to withdraw us from reality, without realizing it, so thinking becomes an addiction especially when we are going through stress.

We don't experience what is going on in our mind through our senses. It is as whatever we think about ceases to exist to our body senses once it is projected in our mind; We experience our thinking through meaning and not through somatic experiences. Or as Alan Watts used to say, those who think too much have nothing to think about other than their own thoughts[1]. Hannah Arendt explained it in her book **The Life of The Mind**: "All thoughts arise out of experiences, but no experience yields any meaning or even coherence without undergoing the operation of imagining and thinking. Seen from the perspective of thinking, life in its sheer thereness is meaningless; seen from the perspective of immediacy of life and the world given to the senses, thinking is, as Plato indicated, a living death" (p87)[2].

Plato associating thinking to a living death was not his negative point of view though. While we are thinking we are unaware of our own corporeality, which Plato understood as achieving our pure soul quality. Plato's philosophical tradition was perpetuated through Europe during the Middle Ages and Renaissance by the Catholic church, influencing philosophers as Descartes who concluded *the soul can think without the body*. This reflects the belief of a duality. The distinction between body and mind (soul)[3].

Against the occidental philosophical tradition is the belief that we think because we have a body; the mind being a product of our body and not distinct from it. Again, thoughts arise out of experiences – from our body senses. As our experiences turn into thoughts the bodily experienced thing disappears to it. As Arendt puts it, "in order to appear in my mind only, it must first be de-sensed, and the capacity to transform sensed-objects into images is called imagination" (p.85). The imagination deals only with what is absent to our senses. The mind deals with nothing other than itself. Perhaps we could say that the opposite of thinking is body experience; perceiving with our senses.

On the other hand, as the Greek philosophers believed, only the spectator and never the actor can see and understand the spectacle of life, because the spectator is free from concerns. The spectator is not acting in the spectacle but only contemplating it. Different from the old occidental philosophical belief, something suggests this contemplation is not done through thoughts and imagination but only through somatic experiences.

I personally believe the best meaning we can give to life is leisure. As Aristotle understood it, it is not the free time we get after a day of work, not a play and not a recreation but the deliberate act of abstaining, of holding oneself back from the ordinary activity determined by our daily wants in order to contemplate it. This contemplation is the act of leisure, "which in turns was the true goal of all others activities, just as peace, for Aristotle, was the true goal of war" – quoting Arendt again.

While for the Greeks the spectator may understand the 'truth' of what the spectacle is about – but with the price of having to pay a withdrawal from participating in it – the oriental wisdom presented by Alan Watts suggests something different; that we can be both the actor and the spectator. As the Taoist story tells, imagine if we were god and knew all without surprises; how boring would it be!? So we play this theater of life for fun – just as children do their play sometimes taking it too serious and forgetting it is just a play – and as we grow older we forget who we are, we forget we are wearing a phony by taking it too serious and thinking it is what we are. The spectator is the one who can see the play and enjoy the spectacle while still playing in it, only knowing, now, that it is all a play and people forgot about it. Like actors playing in a scene for a movie, sometimes taking it too seriously, mistaking the playing character for themselves, or living the character but still knowing they [the actors] are another person behind their characters.

As I understand it, contemplation is the way we can experience what is around us with our body senses, until the moment we gain the awareness about the spectacle we are in, without our thinking distraction that alienates us from our somatic experiences. This is why I think art is important; The thing that makes us stop and listen, see and feel through our senses; paying attention to our somatic experience and step aside from the vicious meanings in thinking.

Truth and meaning are not the same things. Our thinking doesn't bring us the reality truth which we mistake with meanings, because our verbal language, associated with words, is metaphorical and not analogous to the mental images created from our somatic experiences. "Most people have experienced the odd sensation of estrangement that comes from looking long enough at a single object", says Siri Hustvedt in her essay **Ghosts at The Table.** She goes on: "for all of us there was a time before we knew what things were called, and then the world looked different. Cézanne's still life is a rigorous effort to return to a vision unburdened by meaning". In other words, Cézanne's attempt was to see in painting what was lost in language.

When we look, listen and feel hard enough and long enough we contemplate and find a world beyond meaning which tells us something else that our verbal language is too limited to comprise.

1 "It is precise the absence of form and hence of any possibility of intuition [which is a somatic sensation] that characterizes our experience of inner sensation. In Inner experience, the only thing to hold onto, to distinguish something at least resembling reality from incessantly passing moods of our psyche, is persistent repetition." (Arendt, pg40)

2 ARENDT, H. "One / Thinking" in *The Life of the Mind: The groundbreaking investigation on how we think.* New York: Houghton Mifflin Harcourt, 1977.

3 SACKS, O. "Witty Ticcy Ray" in *The Man Who Mistook His Wife for a Hat*. London: Picador, 2011. p.98

MY ATTENTION IS NOT IN TECHNICAL PERFECTIONISM

The photography field attracts many technology and machines enthusiasts who come with the technician attention to it. I see it as one of the reasons for the commercial photography to be seen and used as standard, or reference, for quality among many people interested in photography (although the debate about preferences between realism and rusticity has existed since Ancient Greece and probably even before[1]). The other reason is the fact that commercial photography dominates our visual experience wherever we have contact with publicity[2]. Commercial photographers are mostly technicians who create images based on someone else's ideas. Most of it is technical reproduction and solutions, even the advertised photography in fashion magazines that mimic conceptual fashion photography. Depending on how alienated the photographer is in this approach to photography he may come to the conclusion that what goes beyond such technical and commercial standards is poorly executed or wrong.

Fortunately, photography is not a black and white thing limited to right and wrong. The meaning of anything is in its context. When we talk about quality we have to think about the context and meaning the work has. Commercial photography has its own context and language, and its main purpose is the experience of tangibility; making the product or service presented in the image as tangible to its audience, as if the image viewer can touch and possess the object in the photo with their eyes – The sensual visual appeal. It could not be different when the goal of the image is to sell a sensual joy to people's eyes and stimulate the desires of possession. As John Berger says, in his work **Ways of Seeing**, The publicity image offers an alternative for the public, a better version of themselves, that they can obtain for the price of the product.

Photography that has other purposes will, or should, use other languages; The language that fits its message and context, which can be many. None of them are better or worse than the other, nor more or less correct. Each of them are only good and bad based on their own context, audience and message.

Siri Hustvedt, in her essay **Playing, wild thoughts, and novels underground**, refers to writing in this quote but it actually applies to any kind of artistic work: "There are no rules for writing novels. Those who believe there are rules are pedants and poseurs and do not deserve a minute of our time. Modes of writing and various schools come and go: Grub Street, Naturalism, the nouveau roman, magical realism. The novel remains."

When I photograph I often stay away from the sensual appeal which Cicero in ancient Rome used to call *the corruption of the senses*, because it works in provoking anxieties[3]. Instead, I like to express my feelings and experiences. Technicality is about having control; the technical control of a machine precision appreciated from automated tools, catching our attention to tool settings for the precise controlled result. In order to better express my feelings and experiences I rather let this technical control aside, I take the advantage of the manual control which comes with my spontaneous human touch and failures. Or even when using automated tools, I trust the automated failure as my own human failure with the machine and assuming, therefore, my sincere experience, and adding it to the narrative context where it belongs[4].

"Through perfect nothing we see perfect something"
(Hridaya Sutra)

Brené Brown, who wrote **The Gifts of Imperfection**, explains that it is important to understand the difference between healthy striving and perfectionism. "Healthy striving is self-focused: "How can I improve?" Perfectionism is other-focused: "What will they think?". I think it is important to remember that we should improve in relation to ourselves, in our own language, in our own context and message. Not in relation to a predetermined standard, or have somebody else as reference of improvement as goal and quality. This is not the same as rejecting being inspired by other creators and their works because we all get inspiration from other creators even when unintended, in any way.

At the end I don't want the viewers of my photos seeing themselves transported in the image by provoked anxieties. I want them to take the image as a memory or as a dream that inspires their feelings for them to contemplate their own creative imagination. Or, at least, project something from me in the work which tells who I am, or what we are.

[1][3] GOMBRICH, E.H. *The Preference For The Primitive*. Hong Kong: Phaidon, 2006.

2 BERGER, J. "7" in *Ways of Seeing*. Great Britain: Pinguin Classics, 2008.

4 WATTS, A. "The Yin-Yang Polarity" in *Tao: The Water Course Way*. New York: Pantheon Books, 1975.

28

HUMAN DUALITY INQUIETUDE AND CREATIVE PLEASURE

There is a certain pleasure in executing things that is distinguished [here] in two categories. The first is the pleasure of archiving the end goal and the second is the pleasure in the activity itself. Both, or any activity we start or engage in, is caused by a mental inquietude. Every mental inquietude, according to Antonio Damasio, is caused by somatic experiences; the reaction of the body when we experience irritation, pleasure and everything in between; Reaction as striving for life balance. Our body reacts (emotes) and, from our body reaction, our brain creates mental pictures (icons) of the body reaction experience which we associate to a meaning, and, from which we create feelings. Feelings, then, connect us back to mental pictures activating our memories[1] (of our body experiences; emotions). We like to believe we are rational beings when in fact we are emotional beings[2]. We learn, remember, think and execute things based on mental icons brought by emotions associated with them. Even when we believe we are being purely rational, like in science.

> "There is no pure sensation of anything, not in feeling
> pain, not in tasting wine, and not in looking at art. All
> of our perceptions are contextually coded, and that
> contextual coding does not remain outside us in the

environment but become a psycho-physiological reality within us, which why a famous name attached to a painting literally makes it look better." (Hustvedt, pag20)

We don't perceive the world and reality as it is but as we are; As the mental pictures we have from our experiences and meanings associated to them are. Our five senses are not meant to reveal us to the world out there. They are meant to help us keep the regulation of our life balance (life preservation and perpetuation) such as in finding food when we are hungry, in finding shade when we are tired, in identifying danger to avoid and pleasure to chase. Evolution presented us with our mental capacity in order to quickly, or better, adapt in the short term to our environment changes, increasing our chances of survival and life perpetuation[3]. Nonetheless, we use our highly developed nervous system to attempt the understanding of reality. We can't experience all, or many, mental pictures at once but one by one and, consequently, the feelings associated with each of them one by one – although we can experience them so quickly that we don't realize it[4]. The experience of our mental pictures is linear, which allows us to experience what we call a *train of thoughts*. As we are the tool we use to give meaning to reality we fall in what Kant used to call *The professional thinker fallacy*. We perceive time, reality, history and even science in a linear and progressive way because it is how our mind – and our verbal communication – works; not because reality, time, history and science is linear and progressive. It doesn't mean science does not progress. It means that progress is subjective to our mind[5].

The Will-Power is a mental activity inquietude. Will-Power is not merely the power of choosing or making decisions – it is not a mere desire, strive or wanting. It is rather a conflict between two drives: Yes and No – as Hannah Arendt describes in her book **The Life of The Mind**. The *Will*, before becoming a concept, or a mental organ known by philosophers, was interpreted as a duality in one person, as a hidden second person inside the person. It is as having two "I"s, the "I" who commands and the "I" who obey. The second one perceives both "I"s as a whole willing desire obedience anticipation. The first one is the *Will*. The *Will* is the commanding thought, as described by Heidegger. The *Will* is an attempt to overcome this mental duality conflict[6].

Every mental activity ceases the experience of the senses as well as the experience of our senses ceases our thinking; when we are thinking (having our attention to our mental images and their meanings; train thoughts) we are unaware of our senses perception. If something happens that grabs our attention to our sense perception (our somatic experience; emotion) then we become unaware of our thinking. In order to fulfill the *Will* we act through our senses (act in the world) and once our action is completed it ceases the *Will*, putting us at a mental fulfilling rest – no mental conflict or inquietude but just *being* – because we cease to want things once we have them.

The pleasure from concluding the execution of an activity, that I mentioned at the beginning, comes from the wish against the activity itself, that we do in order to overcome it. The activity is an obstacle to the real goal. It is like the Aristotelian thought that says the goal of work is leisure, as the goal of war is peace. Once you execute the activity and reach its goal you feel fulfilled and at rest, without mental conflict or inquietude (at least for a while).

The second kind of pleasure we have from executing things. The goal is not in the end of the activity but the activity experience itself. Duns Scotus, one of the most original and important philosophers from middle-ages, called it as love; The transformation of the *Will* in love. It is the action that does not need to reach its end in order to bring a restful mind. At the same time, because it never reaches its end it never ceases the *Will*. Thus, the activity causes a temporary pause in the *Will* expectation for an end while still *willing*. Such temporary pause, during the activity, gives us a constant fulfillment; the pleasure in the activity and not in its end. In other words, the activity is not an obstacle to overcome in order to halt the *Will*. The goal is the activity itself.

Coming from a religious philosopher it explains that the divine love, or true love, is the fulfillment one has for a desired object not through possession – which would end the desire – but through pure activities – interaction and creation – around of, or related to, a desired object or goal in general.

Nietzsche interpreted the *Will* is a destructive power. The goal of the *Will* is to become its master, according to him, but once events happen the *Will* has no power; You have no power in shaping the past. Or as in Nietzsche words; The *Will* can not will backwards. For Nietzsche, as well for Heidegger, the desire to have power in past events is the source of our duality conflict (the *Will*). What is left for the frustrated *Will*, for not being the master of past events, is to destroy the past by willing for new events to come – promote changes – in which the *Will* can be the master again.

Ancient Greek philosophers didn't know the *Will* as a mental organ but they had a parable about the best athlete being the one who is not looking for glory or fame – the goal to achieve at the end of the sport activity – but the one who finds the pleasure in the sport itself. Something similar we think today about artists, photographers or creators in general. The true or the best creator being the one not doing it for money or fame but for the art sake. The activity not as a gateway to happiness but the happiness itself. As the Greek philosophers described it, one being both an actor in the stage of life and an spectator of one's own act. The individual duality working together and overcoming its internal duality conflict which causes both body and mind inquietude.

Daoism has a similar allegory about life being a stage where we act, but through our action we forget who we originally are, causing a conflict between our acting character and who we are inside. The conflict is solved when we perceive our acting character and, from such realization, we become our own spectator of our own acting in life, enjoying the stage of life both as actor and as spectator – enjoying the activity by finding fulfillment in it; doing it for its own sake.

In a modernist philosophy this duality is interpreted as the social self and original self (the second called *Being*). The social self hides the internal *Being*. The *Will* is the spontaneous and intuitive pulse of our internal self – our *Being* – emerging during activities focused on the pleasure of the activity's sake, as if enjoying our internal self emerging.

What the Ancient Greek Philosophers and Daoism have in common is the perception of life not as linear but as a cycle. The linear view of life and reality gained space in the west specially because of the way we associate our mental picture and meanings to our linear verbal writing system[7]. The concept of a willing ego is only possible through such a linear view of reality. During the Middle-Ages and Renaissance both linear and cyclical philosophical perception of reality developed parallel to each other; as Hannah Arendt described it: Descartes and Leibniz in one side, Hobbes and Spinoza in the other side and Kant somewhere else. Our scientific path during modernism was influenced by the linear perspective which brought the concept of the willing ego. Such influence was mainly because of a linear religious doctrine imposed by the Catholic Church as a political institution in Europe. As Antonio Damasio narrates in his book **Looking For Spinoza**, he [Spinoza] influenced our great thinkers and discoveries but in a hidden way, behind the linear perception that creates the contradiction between free will and causative effects of a linear event of life. The Inquisition banned any kind of Spinozist philosophy to be learned, used or mentioned for more than one hundred years, consequently – and accidentally – giving more highlight to Descartes philosophy and its influence.

[1, 3, 4] DAMASIO, A. *The strange order of things*: Life, feeling, and the making of cultures. New York: Vintage Books, 2019.

2 HUSTVEDT, S. "Ballon Magic" in A *Woman Looking at Men Looking at Women: Esseys on Art, Sex, and the Mind.* UK: Sceptre, 2016.

5 In the last section of **Critic Of Pure Reason**, Kant claims that man will surely return to metaphysics.

6 *"In the interpretation of Dasein, this structure is something 'a priori'; It is not pieced together, but it is primordially and constantly a whole. It afford us, however, various ways of looking at the items which are constitutive for it. The whole of its structure always comes first; but if we keep it constantly in view, these items, as phenomena, will be made to stand out. And thus we shall have as object for analisys: the world in its worldhood (Chapter 3), Being-in-the-world as Being-with and Being-one's-Self (Chapter 4), and Being-in as such (Chapter 5). By analysis of this fundamental structure, the Being of Dasein can be indicated provisionally. Its existencial meaning is 'care' (Chapter 6)."* HEIDEGGER, M. "Part One: The Interpretation of Temporality, and The Explication of Time As The Trancendental Horizont For The Question Of Being" in *Being And Time.* US: Stellar Classics (Original Edition: 1927) (pag41)

7 *"Every culture is based on assumptions so taken for granted that they are barely conscious, and it is only when we study highly different cultures and languages that we become aware of them. Standard average European (SAE) language, for example, have sentences so structured that the verb (event) must be set in motion by the noun (thing) – thereby posing a metaphysical problem as tricky, and probably as meaningless, as that of the relation of mind and body. We cannot talk of 'knowing' without assuming that there is some 'who' or 'what' that knows, not realizing that this is nothing more than a grammatical convention. The supposition that knowing requires a knower is based on a linguistic and not an external rule, as becomes obvious when we consider that raining needs no reiner and clouding no clouder."* - WATTS, A. *Tao: The Water Course Way.* New York: Pantheon Books, 1975. (p11).

ART AND THE DEPENDENCE ON THE BUREAUCRACY OF TECHNOLOGY

What makes some people suspicious about the *art status* of photography is the fact that the photo creation is highly dependable of a *photo machine*. I heard a couple of years ago about a study by an academic artist saying that photography is not art. His argument was about the technology limitation which the photographer is dependable to create his works.

For decades many photographers have tried to bring photography to the art discussion and galleries to make it more recognized as art. Until nowadays, with many people buying photographs and many photographers calling themselves artists, there are still those who don't consider photography a true art. Or, at least, not as artistic as painting or sculpture.

Recently I saw this question again when somebody wrote in an art community: "When an artist depends on machines (not tools) to create; the machines' capabilities are the controlling factors of the joint creations that comes from the union of artist with machine. An Artist's tools on the other hand can be created by the hand of the artist and is not dependent on the bureaucracy of technology."

It is hard nor to agree with what the quote says. It is right. But when thinking of cameras, are all cameras machines? Digital cameras are certainly pure machines; a body filled with mechanics and electronics in it. But a true camera obscura is just an empty box that can be made with any material, with a hole where the light comes in; which means that it is not a machine at all but just a tool for the photographer as the brush is a tool for the painter.

Photographers can make their own film negative (and positive images), prepare their own plate or paper sensible to light as painters can make their own canvas or any other material they wish to paint on.

Cameras, film negatives and even light have their limitations as canvas and ink have their limitations as well. What makes people feel more like an artist is the ability to craft with a self expression and a vision for their creation in mind. The reason many photographers still use pinhole cameras or film negatives is because they can craft it with their own hands instead of just operating machines that are digital cameras and computers.

Yet, even when highly dependable of the mechanics and digital work and capability, digital photographers and digital artists still can express their creativity and vision through their works. Which I think is what matters after all. Not much different from a director who is dependent from actors' works and abilities, or from contemporary artists who have never touched their creation but paid someone else to build the work setting for them.

It is funny to think about it because before Renaissance artists were not considered artists as they are today. They were just craftermen; hand workers as any other kind of worker.

Is Photography an Easy Way to Make Art?

Photography is not an easier way to make art, it is just easier to have confidence with. We have a natural feeling to find it easier to do things we feel confident doing.

> "While photography is the easiest medium in which to
> be confident it is the hardest medium in which to have
> a distinct personal vision." *(*Chuck Close*)*.

Photography is the easiest form of the art of mimesis; the copy of reality. It is the copy of reality people are usually more attracted to today, and is the copy of reality most people will judge as the parameter for a good quality work.

But when trying to do something else, apart from mimesis, photography can be even more challenging than other forms of art. Because its quite completely copy of reality – especially now a days with digital cameras, that most people don't even need to craft their work in order to have an image ready to print – most people with a camera will be confident they are doing a good photo as soon as they can see a good image quality in their LCD screen. But image quality does not necessarily mean good photo or good art.

To go beyond mimesis it is easier through painting, sculpture, etc, than with photography. It also means the self expression in photography may be more difficult because photographers have to work with real things they photograph instead of creating images straight from imagination and body skills. This is why photography is the hardest medium to have a distinct personal vision.

One does not need much skill to press a button on an automatic camera, to throw paintings or mixing colours on canvas, not even to create shapes in sculptures, as far as the artist can do it with good composition, harmony or even good messages. But photography and other media can demand more skills and craft if you want to make something else.

If you ask a child if painting is easy they will tell you that it is very easy because they feel confident doing so. Until they grow up and they are told that good paintings represent tangible things.

WOMEN, UNWANTED ATTENTION AND SOCIAL PHOBIA

1

If you walk paying attention to how your legs walk, you tend to walk in an awkward way. Your best walk is when you walk unaware of how your legs do it. The same way a painter or a writer will do their paintings and writings in an uncomfortable way if they pay attention to their tools and fingers when they are working. As a photographer I feel that my best photos happen when the camera becomes an extension of my arm, so I don't have to pay much attention to the tool itself which would be in the way of my attention to what I am photographing. Alan Watts exemplifies it by saying that we know when the shoes or belt we are wearing is conformable when we walk and forget about them. If the shoes or any other accessory on us keep reminding us about themselves – catching our attention because we feel something about it – it means they are not comfortable and then becomes a distraction; in the way of our attention to other things and to our spontaneity. The very same happens with self-awareness. When we are self-aware – the attention to oneself before any other attention, reminding us about who we are, what we are doing and how we are doing whatever we are doing – we become uncomfortable in ourselves and we start acting and feel awkward, because we have our attention on our body position, body movements and its many meanings. It is watching ourselves as if in the eyes of others, who may be watching us, that blocks our spontaneity. This is why the best actors are the ones who forget they are acting, by stopping watching what they are doing as if in the eyes of another person – spectators in a theater, for example – and they become or incorporate their characters' acting, feeling the character pains and pleasures as their own as actors. Otherwise the acting looks fake, artificial, awkward, or simply acting.

2

Women – especially young attractive ones – often suffer the stress of unwanted attention. Even worse when it turns into catcalling. You get the awareness of the dirty eyes from others on you. When one gets too much of it it becomes toxic, polluting their attention and mood. We know that many men catcall because they know, or have a high expectation, that women and others around them will not react and confront them, or repress them, about it. They feel an individual freedom to do it, as well as a cultural freedom, or duty as a proof to others and themselves that they are men, a *real man*; They don't expect obtaining anything from it other than asserting their masculinity.

Years ago, when I was with a friend walking in the streets of Israel, I noticed a beautiful woman who my eyes felt hypnotized at but I only became aware of my gaze when I noticed she was acting uncomfortable so I quickly looked away from her. I told my friend how uncomfortable and unhappy I feel when I make women feel uncomfortable with my attention. He told me that, as a man, I am not supposed to be ashamed of making women uncomfortable, otherwise it shows them I am insecure and women like men who are confident and dominant in attitude, such as looking at a woman with no shame when attracted to her, according to him. And he is right, but only when the woman feels attracted to the gazing man;

so she wants his attention.

If a man is confident and spontaneous it shows the target woman that he believes he has something to offer and that he has experiences which lead to his confidence. It can be confirmed that one really has what to offer, in the eyes of others around him, when the person is surrounded by friends, specially surrounded by other women; The people who are enjoying his *acting power*, as Frederic Lordon calls it in his book **Willing Slaves of Capital**. Eventually, his confidence ends up convincing someone that he has indeed something to offer while at the same time he is also always risking putting some women in an uncomfortable situation, for them not being interested in the man asserting his *power*. His act is not only to convince other people about his *acting power* but to convince himself before anyone else, about having such power. Especially nowadays with the motivational culture of *"believing in yourself"* and *"fake until you make it"*.

A man may be more conscious and cautious in order to make sure women who he interacts with feels completely safe and comfortable, who consequently may feel more comfortable around him, but he risks of being over cautious with a woman who may be interested on him and expecting a confident, dominant, doubtless attitude from him towards her, that if not shown he becomes an insecure man to her – A socially not man enough because for society a real man is always sure about himself, about what he does, about what they he has offer without fear of being rejected; otherwise he risks of being defined as lacking affection, lacking attention and love pleasures.

> "The social presence of a woman is different in kind
> from that of a man. A man's presence is dependent
> upon the promise of power which he embodies. If the

promise is large and credible his presence is striking.
If it is small and incredible, he is found to have little
presence. The promised power may be moral,
physical, temperamental, economic, social, sexual –
but its object is always exterior to the man. A man's
presence suggests what he is capable of doing to you
or for you. His presence may be fabricated, in the
sense that he pretends to be capable of what he is not.
But the pretense is always towards a power which he
exercises on others.

By contrast, a woman's presence expresses her own
attitude towards herself, and defines what can and
cannot be done to her."[1] (BERGER, p39)

3

Robert Levenson did a long study with couples emotion finding
that the longer the allele in serotonin transport gene the less
sensitive the person is to the environment's emotional stimulus,
while the shorter the allele the more sensitive is the person to
emotional stimulus. If we place two individuals in a situation that
stimulates them to feel happy and then sad, the person with shorter
allele will react more to such stimulus, feeling more happy and
then more sad than the person with the longer allele. It could be the
reason why people's mood and atmosphere around me causes a
great effect on my mood as well. So if I feel a person is feeling
uncomfortable it makes me feel uncomfortable as well, such as the
woman who I was gazing at in the streets of Tel Aviv. If I am not
wrong, I guess we can call it empathy, the counter-transference of
putting yourself in the other person's shoes, thus feeling as the

other person feels or may be feeling.

I watched a documentary about Incels (self-denominating involuntary celibates men) and what got my attention the most was when the teacher, in the documentary, said that Incels are not merely feeling sexually frustrated but feeling socially excluded – because sexual pleasure is the fastest and easiest way to materialize and compensate the feeling expression of lacking emotional, social or, very often, maternal affection, among other forms of lack of affection. I used to believe that women are more or less friendly to men as a reaction to how men approach women, conditioning women behavior – of feeling safe or unsafe, comfortable or uncomfortable. It may be true to a certain point and places but it is not an universal law, it varies from place to place and from people to people. After living and moving among different countries and cultures I came to realize it's a vicious cycle, with men and women conditioning each other. I can tell that where women are friendly, even when rejecting men approach, men tend to accept the rejection better because they don't feel segregated or humiliated but socially accepted and understood. The contrary, with aloofness, scare or disgust women or any human being can cause people to feel irritated, because it means social segregation to them, as if you are treating others inferior than you and it makes people feel not accepted socially – with their act seen as not understood and so not welcomed for the social joy. Some people may say they only need to grow thick skin and "brush it out" to overcome how one makes them feel, but it's easier to judge people as over sensitive when the one who is judging have close friends or a family to act and interact with, from which they have a sense of belonging in this world. Otherwise one feels alienated, displaced, and the number of people aging in solitude is growing as never before. Catcalling is often a desperate desire to socially interact, to obtain attention and to brush away any question about their own sexuality (identity) for feeling segregated – not understood.

4

According to WHO (World Health Organization) solitude is a disease nowadays. As social animals being alone, which causes people to feel segregated, causes us emotional distress with side effects worse than smoke and drinking. Lonely people have a shorter life expectancy, higher risk of heart diseases and higher chances of developing cancer, all because of the distress of feeling socially excluded[2].

Some Americas were saying in a social media that they are over stressed because they work too long hours. Which is true but in Europe, such as in Nordic countries and especially in Germany, people are also often easily over stressed despite working less hours. I believe it is because people do not like to interact with strangers. When you feel apart (alienated) from others around you feel hostile. When I first arrived in Germany I was not much bothered by women in supermarket counters turning their face away from me when I was paying for my groceries, without me doing any kind of verbal or visual interaction with them. Later I noticed that some women also turn their back to me when I am being introduced to their friend's cycle. Also when stepping in public transport, I noticed women looking angry at me for apparently no reason at all, they all seemed in disturbed. I thought, at first, it was some kind of xenophobia and it actually is to a certain extent, when you feel socially alienated and afraid of people because they are foreigners or just different. When one feels disconnected from strangers, feeling as having to be careful about them. Talking about it, it was confirmed to me that women in Germany do it for precaution; just in case I, as a man, flirt with them. Such kind of misandry is not only accepted by German society but expected as part of their culture – of *being direct*. Whenever I talk about it people tell me that it will never change, that it is their culture or that is just *women things* – implying that I have to forget about it and pretend everybody is doing fine – despite the fact I have never experienced anything like it anywhere else I have been other than in Germany. To me it is like saying that it is ok to be racist or antisemitic *just in case*, and that it should be accepted because it is a cultural thing. I don't agree with it and I don't like double standards. I will never change a cultural fear and behaviour indeed, specially because people refuse to talk about it. It is not only bad for men who suffer misandry but also for women, because if women behave like this it means they fear others as having the potential of being highly hostile against them, even in one of the most safe places in the world that is Germany.

5

I see people burning out for small stupid things that could be easily solved with a little talk. But people hesitate and avoid talking because they are afraid of others' reaction, creating a kind of social phobia. Instead, people expect to conform, expecting everyone to conform to certain behaviours and agreeing to things which help them not need to talk and interact with others. If you don't conform people show their reprehension with dirty looks and other kinds of frustrating reactions, and, in such social control, you feel hostile. Little mistakes are not acceptable and it frustrates people for having to deal with strangers. The Nordics like to blame their grumpiness and social isolation on the weather but in Ireland and Canada, it seems, people are much more relaxed and easy even with their dark winters and wet weather, because they have a more liberal culture (I am using the "liberal" word not in a political meaning here). They don't feel alienated from people.

6

There are two kinds of freedom because there are two kinds of self in every person: the individual and the social, each of them limiting the freedom of the other to a certain extent. People talk a lot about freedom today but If not considering the two kinds of freedom the talk is just a no sense ideological sophism. Social freedom means safety from others in society according to Montaigne, which requires a certain control and limitation (responsibility) on the individual freedom. If you want a total individual freedom you are being against social freedom (individual safety from others in society). Despite the nihilists one of the main reasons, if not the main reason, we live in society and think society is for the individual safety sake.

We live in a society of control, which Deleuze described to be in gradual change from what Foucault called Disciplinary society. The disciplinary society may not be completely vanished yet but many of its characteristics we find still strong in more conservative societies. Although Germany has a very liberal approach to individual affairs, the German social conduct and mentality to changes, which they are averse to, are very conservative. So we can still find strong characteristics of a disciplinary society in Germany, that is based on social hierarchical observation, normalizing judgment and examination that induce people to control their behaviour to a standardized conformity.

The disciplinary society means that people have the duty to observe everyone's behaviour. This is why in Germany it is normal and a cultural thing to stare – or give long gazes – to others in the streets. If you act differently people watch you, not as spectators but as judges, because you are supposed to conform. It is important and kind of funny to have to tell that most Germans are not even consciously aware about it for being oblivious, but unconsciously they react to it the same way a person who claims to not like Picasso's paintings but, despite their claims, somatically they react otherwise without realizing it. It means that both men and women experience unwanted attention and suffer the natural human distress about it, of feeling constantly observed and consequently behaving awkwardly and in introversion – which Germans are well aware of and they consider it part of their cultural personality, although not questioning its causes – for watching themselves as in the eyes of others and not being able to be spontaneous; since spontaneity is only possible with individuality. Consequently, as part of a conformity as a duty, you are not expected to question much but to accept it – to conform. Questions are often seen as an attempt to not accept, to not conform, to break the rules, to promote changes or simply to stand out from the crowd – with an individuality.

Conformity seems to be part of another psychological aspect: Identity. Before Nation-States people had their identities associated with ethnics; the use of ethnicity to judge other individuals based on a supposed natural tendencies of their ethnic qualities and vices. Some countries today, like in Germany, strongly kept some aspects of it. Reason why we find so many people born in Germany who are from second or third generation of immigrant families who are still being seen and called as Turkish, Italians, Portugueses, etc. The concept of nationality came with Enlightenment values that every person has to be seen as equal and responsible for their own individual success and failures, which required the formation of Nation-States where the political body would be apart from the social body. From Nation-States comes nationality, under which one is supposed to be seen not as belonging to an ethnical value but is supposed to be seen as equal under the law, included in the society identity regardless of their blood origin. Many countries in Europe conserved the tradition of seeing the individual not as mere individual belonging to the nation but as an individual belonging, before anything else, to an ethnicity – its supposed natural mentality, qualities and vices – conformity; The mentality of people who try to know you by asking you where you are from and what your profession is before trying to know and understand you as an individual. To conform is a way to feel belonging to a group, as being socially included, as have its identity. In such a view, when questioned about one's social conforming and group perspectives they feel as if their identity is being attacked.

7

But why it is so hard for people to perceive it? The reason is because, along with it all, there is the social willful blindness[3]. Oliver Sacks narrates that Tourette's syndrome used to be well reported with many known cases, with a rich literature from its discovery in 1885 until the end of its century. Charcot, Freud, Babinski and Tourette (the syndrome discoverer) were among the last of professionals with a combined vision of soul and body, the "it" and the "I", in neurology and psychiatry. At the turn of the century, professionals started to interpret the "I" (the mind) as independent, or apart, from the "it" (the body). The soulless neurology and bodiless psychology. In this change, not only the understanding of Tourette's syndrome disappeared but the syndrome itself had disappeared as well. No more reported cases and no more literature about it. It was interpreted as extinct. Many doctors even thought the past literature were mythical reports of naive and imaginative professionals from the past, because they could not be converted in the new framework tradition of 20th century neuroscience and psychology. Oliver Sacks claimed to have never seen a patient with Tourette's syndrome, until in 1971 when he published an essay about Tics in the *Washington Post*.

Many people who read it wrote to Oliver Sacks telling him that they have the symptoms he had described in the essay. After visiting one of his correspondents Sacks realized that the man he went to visit had Tourette's syndrome. Not only that, after the visit Oliver Sacks could easily identify many people in the streets of New York with Tourette's syndrome by only walking home and from home to work.

Often, when I try to talk about such subjects, many Germans tell me that they don't stare but they just look a little longer to others and there is nothing wrong about it. But then, why women behave in such distress and men have apprehensive manners? Because of the lack of talking and awareness it seems to me that women think they are the only ones being gazed at, and men are the only ones gazing at, as if it is (only) a *man thing* and not a German culture thing. It is half funny and half depressing consciously experiencing every day being stared at by women which causes me to naturally look back at them, because it is what we do when we feel there are eyes watching us. But when I look back at them they react in distress as if I have any interest on them in particular, as if I am being a *toxic man* when in fact they are unaware that they have been inconveniently staring at me first. When I avoid looking back, pretending I don't notice they are looking at me, their stares become even stronger, longer and more discomforting, because we know they are not looking and judging with good eyes. I am a visual disturbance of conformity.

8

I am not suggesting that the privatization of a social problems is exclusive to Germanic culture, it is actually an industry which by ignoring a problem that is social people are induced to believe that is not the society that has to change but you, as individual, who has a problem for feeling affected and reacting negatively to society's problems, convincing people to join classes and buy materials for meditation, going to experts talking about self-improvement, buying self-help books and even convincing people that they need to do more sports. Meditation and sports are good for personal health, but not good when used as tools to ignore that people's stress is a social condition and not an individual problem.

A lot of Germans – at least in the internet, which is a small group that does not represent the nation as a whole – get really irritated and aggressive against me when I touch such subjects, because they convince themselves that I am being against their culture and consequently their country, when in fact my allele in serotonin transport gene may probably be way too short. Feeling the heavy atmosphere among women – and men – in distress, storming reacting or in fear for no apparent reason affects me and I am not oblivious about it. I can't help thinking about it trying to understand it – as I try to understand societies, humans and life in general – and hope for its eventual change, although I don't have much faith in changes. I don't have anything against the culture or the country but I care about people's well being regardless of culture, ethnicity and nationality. Especially my well being. I don't like to ignore the problem pretending it is an individual problem. It is a social problem that people may try to ignore in order to conform, but somatically people can not ignore it.

1 BERGER, J. "3" in *Ways of Seeing*. Great Britain: Pinguin Classics, 2008.

2 *Social isolation, loneliness in older people pose health risks*. National Institute on Aging. https://www.nia.nih.gov/news/social-isolation-loneliness-older-people-pose-health-risks . April 23,2019

3 SACKS, O. "Witty Ticcy Ray" in *The Man Who Mistook His Wife for a Hat*. London: Picador, 2011.

THE ECONOMICS OF JOY OR THE STRIVE FOR BALANCE

We photographers, or any creative and art lovers, have a lot in common with those in love with business and money. Despite the criticism and sometimes conflicting attitude among our differences, often resulting in the feeling of being against each other, we are looking for the same through different means.

Either if we care about it or not we can't deny that society is highly driven by money, status, aesthetics and so on. Values; that are related to the power of influence. The influence to create and the influence of attracting people persuaded to collaborate with us for our creation. Collaboration that people offer as exchange of some of the access to such values, which once acquired enough it gives them the power to create and influence as well.

We know about people who have the belief that human interaction has only one meaning, and that would be money (which all other values would be related to). In this particular perspective, money is what defines you. Your abilities, your brightness, your position in society, your level of access to goods and services, and your level of creative power. There is a truth in it, not for natural reasons but for cultural reasons. The only way to survive with a healthy and integrated life balance in today's society is by acquiring money – Which, ironically, the stress and worries related to money often scorn our health and life balance. The amount of money needed will depend on values and views of those around you, I suppose.

What I disagree with in this view is about money being the means of every human relation. It is the meaning for social integration at a certain level but not the meaning of human interaction. Humans, as any alive organism, strive for survival and, according to Antonio Damasio, such survival is measured by the organism's balance[1]. We have the perception of balance through emotions; Visible or invisible somatic action and movements in reaction to something that provoked them. We perceive what causes us joy or irritability – and anything in between – through our body reaction according to what stimulates it. In short, we build emotional (somatic reaction) defenses against what causes us distress and emotional attachment to what causes us joy, in order to maintain a balance for life preservation and perpetuation. Simple living organisms such as insects, mono-cellular and even bacteria don't have consciousness of their emotions – which is not the same as feelings. Only animals who have feelings (mental icons produced by a developed brain) can feel what they emote, which require a more developed nervous system. As Antonio Damasio simplify in a short quote, "emotions play in the theater of the body. Feelings play in the theater of the mind".

We can then conclude that the meaning of human interaction is Joy. Even if the job we work with is not joyful we do it for the payment, normally through monetary earning. Money brings us a joyful feeling, not because of the money itself but because of the joyful things – and people – we can obtain through it. And the most joyful thing one can have is to contemplate oneself as the cause of joy to others[2], according to Frédéric Lordon.

"Since this [joy] is renewed as man considers his

virtues, or his power of acting, everyone is anxious to
tell his own deeds, and show off his powers, both of
body and mind." - (Lordon)

During my early adulthood I was often taking the buses in front
of the building where I used to live. As normally, at least for me, I
had always been ignored. Not disrespected but just ignored. At
least until I started attending a flight attendant course that imposed
on me a formal look and behaviour. When I left home for the first
time wearing a suit and tie – in such an elegant and status symbol
outfit – was when I noticed I had people's attention, servitude and
privileged treatment. Bus drivers welcoming with "good morning
sir", shop attendants looking forward to serve me first and women,
who usually would avoid contact and interaction with me, were
now smiley and welcoming approachable. I was the same poor guy
as before, only that I was in fancy clothes going to and returning
from a fancy neighborhood. The talk about the social prejudice in
Brazilian society back then was still a kind of taboo among many
people, despite today's obviousness, but it was a clear fact I
deduced from my experience. Such experience made me feel good
about myself but I could not just ignore the fact that people were
treating me based on a belief they have about me that wasn't true,
based on my clothes symbolism. A belief in my power of acting,
my power of providing joy to others – biological and social
harmony satisfaction – which they wished to acquire from me.

In 2008 I arrived in Ireland where I met great photographers
and models who, thanks to them, I could learn from, build my
portfolio with and get some jobs as photographer through. Overall,
excluding some exceptions, we were not looking for money or
status in a direct way but looking for fun – have joy. Models,
makeup artists and photographers among other creators were happy

to be part of projects for the creativity and joy sake, that consequently helped us in further opportunities in our respective industries. Enjoying and respecting each other's work without snobbish attitudes, aloofness, or competition about who has the privilege to be the joy provider to others (the center of attention and importance), agreeing that we share joy among us, making we all feeling in harmony working with each other – a biological (consequently emotional) and social harmony balance. We were all offering and acquiring the power of acting from each other without the monetary gate keeping. Money? it always could be negotiated according to what we could afford. I was paying my bills working in a convenience store which was fine. My time in Ireland was the most joyful and prolific in my life, all that required little money but only trust. I found models searching among students at a local university and I met many people through street photography.

Money is the value that gives us the power of acting, but we must not forget that the value we give to money is not in the money itself but in the power of creation, of acting, that money provides and restricts – gatekeeping. This is the joy we are after and to truly obtain such joy it requires trust. Otherwise, the joy of monetary power becomes a monopoly that creates envy and segregation. Consequently it creates social stress. John Berger says that the happiness of being envied is called glamour[3].

> "Being envied is a solitary form of reassurance. It depends precisely upon *not sharing your experience with those who envy you.* You are observed with interest but you do not observe with interest – if you do, you will become less enviable. In this respect the envied are like bureaucrats; the more impersonal they are, the greater the illusion (for themselves and for others) of their power. The power of the glamorous

resides in their supposed happiness: the power of the bureaucrat in his supposed authority." — (BERGER, pag.127)

I arrived in Germany with the expectation to continuous the photography lifestyle I had in Ireland but I was wrong about it. Making contacts became rare for me, everybody is looking for money even though they don't need it. Being able to offer joy through my work became not enough because people are not interested in sharing joy but in monopolizing it through monetary status and closed social cycle, using the money status as gatekeeping, as a trust symbol. Even among models and creators who look for no payment in collaborative work, they often are looking for photographers who show to have fancy tools, a dedicated studio in a fixed address. It doesn't matter to them the result and the joy of the activity unless it can be provided through monetary status, as the access to a monopolized joy which they can justify their aloofness and segregation.

It also results in – or is a consequence of – a social fear, a distrust of people who look for joy sharing without segregation, for being suspicious of them as if they have second intentions; The intention to steal something maintained through the monetary gate-keeping – the illusion of a bureaucratic power. Those who try to detour the money barrier are seen as segregated from the privilege of a monopolistic joy; the ones who lack acting power – money in this case – and consequently are seen as having not much to provide as a joy. They are seen as desperate to take the monetary monopolistic power from those who have it.

Models and photographers seem to compete on their self importance, on who is the joy provider to the other, instead of enjoying it as an exchange through helping each other for the same joyful result as a goal. People are not approachable because they distrust strangers' attempt to join in, as if attempting to obtain monetary or sexual gains from them – when not, they see such strangers as mad because they are not used to seeing social relations beyond monetary and status values. To be sure, it is interpreted that outsiders' attempt of interaction can only be about the dubious intention of climbing and becoming a competitor as the joy provider in a monopolistic culture kept through monetary – and sexual – threshold.

I think the key is empathy and so the understanding of what really matters, what we are striving for. We are striving for balance that comes with joy. Through such understanding I suppose we can learn the importance of trust and honesty required for us to be able to enjoy life and society together. Because *Being envied is a solitary form of reassurance.*

1 DAMASIO, A. *The strange order of things*: Life, feeling, and the making of cultures. New York: Vintage Books, 2019.

2 LORDON, F. *Willing Slaves Of Capital: Spinoza and Marx on Desire*. London: Verso, 2014

3 BERGER, J. "7" in *Ways of Seeing*. Great Britain: Pinguin Classics, 2008.

THE POWER OF ACTING AND TRUST

"Nothing would mean anything if I didn't have a life of use to others", says Angelina Jolie.

Oliver Sacks said we are our internal self-narrative; The narrative we describe our experiences, our acting and our feelings. Without an internal self-narrative we have no identity; we don't know who we are[1].

We become ourselves through others who we interact with, who we share experiences, feelings and emotions with shaping our experiences[2]. The self is always touched by the otherness. It is about finding or identifying the self in the other person, according to Susan Sontag, who we recognize their features, mood, feelings, culture, beliefs and acting within ourselves[3]. We can literally say that plurality is the law of the earth, without the other we are left alone with our thoughts and living solely in reflection creates insatiable desires[4]; the endless pursuit to fill an emptiness (a biological unbalance) and feed a starved self-image, says Hannah Arendt. An urge to act because only through acting we can feel real and fulfilled. Experiences nurture our senses and through it is born the *Self*, says Frédéric Lordon, who describes it as the *economics of joy*[5].

Empathy is the ability to put ourselves in others' shoes so we become kind and honest to others as if we were doing it for ourselves, because we are feeling how it is to be in another person's position. This causes the brain to produce serotonin, that makes us have a well-being feeling. The same when someone is kind and honest to us, we have the empathy to put ourselves in their shoes and we understand they are putting themselves in our shoes, allowing them to feel good in such expression towards us. For our brain it means we are socially understood and understanding symbolizes acceptance. It is the cause of a social and biological harmony because from others acceptance and understanding comes self-reassurance and self-acceptance. But we can also call it love – Agape love to be more precise; The highest form of Christian love – that we can have towards friends, neighbors and even strangers. But if people feel alienated from each other in society it causes an opposite feeling and reaction called cynicism.

Empathy, social confidence and play are strongly related. Play is embedded not only in humans but in all kinds of animals; Fish, lizards, spiders, birds, they all play. It was found that play is part of evolution and it is as important as sleeping and eating, according to scientist Stuart Brown. Animals that grow up playing have more social confidence and social intelligence, more empathy even towards other species and they become less aggressive by showing less signs of violence, being more relaxed. Some animals, such as rats, become depressed if hindered from playing. When growing up without playing animals and humans develop social anxieties[6].

Play is universal, part of every human being's creativity and the source of a meaningful life. The capacity to add something of one's own to the common world is the most elementary form of human creativity[7]. If such capacity is destroyed – which can happen for many reasons, such as economic isolation, social isolation or cultural isolation – isolation becomes all together unbearable, according to Arendt again.

Happiness is found in joy. We have joy in things that make us feel a biological and social harmony[8]. The biggest joy one can have is to appreciate oneself as the cause of joy to others, which gives the person a great power of acting and interaction (socially acceptance or the sense of belonging)[9]. Unfortunately, in our society, there is a big competition for that power through glamour, popularity, money, fame, status, etc; things that cause the monopolization of joy, the monopolization of the acting power, the limitation of social integration and harmony. Consequently, from such monopolization comes hate, blames, humiliation, envy, jealousy and further distress people cause to each other. It also includes exploitation of people, or submission to people, looking for the integration by overcoming the social gate-keeping threshold, since being social is a biological necessity. Aloofness is the bureaucratic self image, or illusion, of a social power of belonging and the power of being a gatekeeper of social belonging.

Acting and playing mean appearing. To appear involves confidence and risk, both that comes from trust. Trust we find where we identify ourselves with, otherwise the other feels alien to us. When the otherness appears as alien to us we feel judged, excluded, hatred, cynic and not being able to act because of anxieties caused by such feelings. Consequently, not being able to become; not being able to build an "I", said Alan Watts. The monopolization of joy through money, aloofness and even culture alienates people, causing them to feel excluded from the social and biological harmony.

The conclusion is that having fun is a serious matter. Through acting and playing we develop imagination which is important for us to gain a wider perspective of our reality, from our senses' nurture, which makes us less alienated or less averse to different things and people.

So love people for letting you express your empathy and let them express their empathy. Attention is the kindest act a person can give to another. We are not supposed to take life and people too seriously but play with them and then let them go; moving on with changes in life and its realities. We have to be grateful for the experience of moments we get from people and the nice memories they helped us to stamp in our self-narrative, that forms our sense of identity. We should be grateful to have another person who accepts us for such exchange, for our social and biological harmony, because it demands trust above all.

At the end we are all the same only in different circumstances. Thank you for your trust in my act, that gives me a self-narrative about who I am and where I belong to, which without I would not be able to find my *Self* and there would be no "I".

1 SACKS, O. "The Lost Mariner" in *The Man Who Mistook His Wife for a Hat.* London: Picador, 2011.

[2][4][7] ARENDT, H. *The Life of the Mind: The groundbreaking investigation on how we think.* New York: Houghton Mifflin Harcourt, 1977

6 Brown S. M. Jr.; Vaughan C. *Play: How it Shapes the Brain, Opens the Imagination, and Invigorates the Soul.* New York: Avery, 2009

8 SONTAG, S. "The Antropologist as Hero" in *Against Interpretation: And Other Essays.* London: Pinguin Clasics, 2009.

[5][9] LORDON, F. *Willing Slaves Of Capital: Spinoza and Marx on Desire.* London: Verso, 2014

9 DAMASIO, A. *The strange order of things: Life, feeling, and the making of cultures.* New York: Vintage Books, 2019.

CERTAINTY AND THE STRIVING FOR RECOGNITION IN A SOCIETY WHERE IDENTITY IS EPHEMERAL

There are things we hide from ourselves and we are not aware of; they are kept in our unconsciousness. At the same time we express them through or activities, speech and feelings that generate our thoughts but we still remain unaware of them. Even if somebody points it out to us we tend to not recognize what we are hiding from ourselves, and there is an emotional reason for it. What people want to deny the most in a debate is the evidence they are being emotional rather than rational. As demonstrated by Antonio Damasio, in his book **The Strange Order of Things**, we are essentially emotional and not as rational as we like to believe.

Many people are starving for recognition. The reason for this is because identity is ephemeral in a society where we can dream of, and pursue to, become whatever we want. Otto Rank described the past civilizations with a strong sense of belonging and identity through their activities. Back then people normally continued to live in the same community where their families had been for generations, working in the same field and business that their families had for generations as well, without ever thinking of, or dreaming about, to become an aristocrat or a noble. Each social group, and their relation to their jobs, had their own distinct psychology, mentality, behavior, fashion and culture, where individuals tended to bound together. This distinct social characteristic is where they would always find their sense of belonging and identity[1]. People were recognized by their work and community. David Harvey goes further, by presenting how the land of a community and its landscape is strongly related to the individual's sense of identity. It justifies the socialist workers' unions, in a deteriorated industrial economy, fighting to keep their unhealthy jobs as well as polluting industries in their community – conflicting with globalists socialists[2]. Because without it they feel they are losing something about themselves; The sense of identity and belonging that they get from such activities and landscape, because it is where and what their entire community have been living and working through all their lives[3]. With the development of capitalism, and consequently the rise of the bourgeois psychology, as Hannah Arendt had described it, the nationalistic sense of equality[4], as the dominant social ideology[5], influenced people to move from their communities and from their traditional activities to cities, looking for better economic opportunities in different jobs – also losing their "knowhow" with the development of technology and specialization. The result is the crisis of identity we find in society today[6].

Our identity is presented through our expression and every expression is a message to another real or imaginary person (sometimes our own selves). Siri Hustvedt explains that there is no "I" without an "other" because the feedback of others is what makes me perceive and know who I am[7]. Since we can go after whatever we want to be, by chasing down the best job opportunities and neighborhood to live in, we need constant feedback about what we become. Or even worse, the confirmation that we are accomplishing the success of our personality, archiving our dreams that are related to our identity, which is confirmed only by people's recognition. When a person still feels insecure about their accomplishments and recognition they pretend – to other people and to ourselves – they are successful and confident about themselves. People pretend to have the recognition or accomplishment they don't have as a way of convincing everybody – and even oneself – that it is true; calling those who don't recognize their supposed successful personality as envious, for being afraid of them to reveal what one has been hiding – their fragile image. By pretending the person can play it as if it is true and, consequently, they feel it is true, often convincing people and even oneself it is true, even if deep inside, in their unconsciousness, they know it is not true.

John Berger, in **The ways of Seeing**, shows how glamour was born; The acquisition of a personality's image that other people wish to have. The aloofness is the bureaucrat attitude of those who are the gatekeeper of social recognition and, consequently, social integration – the group acceptance that gives a person the sense of belonging – through images, as described by Frédéric Lordon in **Willing Slaves of Capital**. The pretending is in order to not feel excluded, as an attempt to protect oneself from feeling miserable, for being partially or totally excluded from a group recognized as successful by today's society.

The biggest fear of any bureaucrat is to lose their power that is always imaginary. A power that is imaginary comes with insecurity. Certainty is the tool insecure people have in order to convince themselves about who they are. They have to believe that what they are is absolute. They need to believe in the absolute in order to overcome their insecurities.

In a debate we talk about our opinions, knowledge and beliefs, but these three things are not just data that we put in and take out our minds; they are identity. Identity is related to people's cognitive experiences because the brain does not compute; it emotes. What we have as truth is from what we trust. Trust we get from what we identify ourselves with; as being from what we belong to or wish to belong to. For this reason, insecurity tends to make many people believe that opinions, knowledge and beliefs are absolute. Or even worse, it makes people believe that science is absolute. When one believes something is absolute they do not need to question it ever – and they will not like if somebody else questions it. Questioning something the person believes to be absolute is for them as if others are questioning his identity. Changing opinions or point of view demands a changing of how you perceive and identify yourself with the subject, which literally means changing who you are. The person who looks for absolutism does not want changes because changes are the cause of insecurities they hide behind their absolutist beliefs.

Many people want to believe that science and logic are absolute so they can convince themselves that their supposed absolutist beliefs are scientific and logical. So they can use personal attacks on the identity of those who question them and their absolutist beliefs as no logic or no sense. But science is the opposite of absolute because reality is in constant movement and in constant change. So it requires the person to keep always questioning, challenging and changing what they believe to be their knowledge in order to gain and grow their knowledge forwards. Certainty does not allow it. If one questions the thing believed to be "the truth", they may not be certain about such "truth". They may not be certain about his absolutist views, and such uncertainty exposes insecure people to their own fears.

At the end, most people tend to research what confirms their bias, what they strongly identify themselves with, often pretending they are looking for knowledge when in fact they are looking for their certainty confirmation. Absolutism is not for people who want knowledge but certainty, as the David Bowie 's *Law* song narrates.

Certainty is for people looking for control and so power (on themselves, on a groups of people or on society). The faith of an absolutist rule that will not allow things to change – so people believe. Every search for control, morality and rules comes out of fear. The fear of the unpredictable spontaneity. The desire to force reality and nature to adapt to them instead of adapting themselves to reality and nature symbiosis, with the belief they have the absolutist knowledge and science to impose their wishes upon nature and reality.

The Greeks dedicated many of their narratives to this theme. It's called Tragedy; Stories about heroes who try to run from their fate but they can not. Greek Tragedies teach us about our incapacity to control reality's symbiosis[8]. A symbiosis that we are not able to fully understand. More than that, it is good that we can not control it because it is the over control of it that breaks life and nature symbiosis, so shifting times come as the symbiosis owns self regulation.

If we understand it we become able to stop blaming people for the changes in society, for changes in their groups and changes in ourselves that make us so insecure. Then, we better can recognize our insecurities and fears because we become more honest with ourselves and with other people. Through honesty we start to identify ourselves with people around us and find comfort in them – which constitutes heaven. Feeling belonging instead of feeling the fear of social segregation; The fear of having to bear our fate on our own that constitutes hell. The fear of not belonging in a society of ephemeral identity.

1 RANK, O. *Psychology and The Soul*. Mansfield Centre: Martino Publishing, 2011

2 HARVEY, D. "Militant Particularism and Global Ambition" in *The Ways Of The World*.

London: Profile Books, 2017.

3 HARVEY, D. "The Nature of Environment: The Dialectic of social and Environmental Change" in *The Ways Of The World*. London: Profile Books, 2017.

4 ARENDT, H. "The Jews and Society" in *Origins of Totalitarianism*. UK: Pinguin Classics, 2017.

5 RANK, O. *Beyond Psychology*. New York: Dover, 1958.

6 ARENDT, H. "Ideology and Terror: A Novel Form of Government" in *Origins of Totalitarianism*. UK: Pinguin Classics, 2017. (see page 370)

7 HUSTVEDT, S. "Becoming Others" in *A Woman Looking at Men Looking at Women: Esseys on Art, Sex, and the Mind*. UK: Sceptre, 2016.

8 RANK, O. *The Mith of The Birth of The Hero: A Psychology Interpretation of Mytology*. Mansfield Centre: Martino Publishing, 2011.

INDIVIDUAL PSYCHOLOGICAL CONFLICTS AND THE DOMINANT SOCIAL ORDER IDEOLOGY

1

Ideology; everybody has one if you understand that ideology is just a set of ideas and beliefs that is based on the individual, or a group, psychology and behaviour rationalization, and which is not necessarily a good or bad thing[1].

Every country and society has many ideologies. Among them one emerges as the dominant one, which will impose its psychology and behaviour based on its understanding of what is acceptable and what is "normal"; what makes sense from the point of view of one's own psychology – and which may not make sense to others' psychology, since truth is only a measure defined by a set of parameters that allow us to interpret our own limiting understanding of a complex rich reality, and such parameters will vary according to different ideologies and their psychologies.

People in every society will tend to fit in the dominant psychology and behaviour – even if it is not originally their own psychology and behaviour – in order to fit in the social expectations and standards, wishing to become socially accepted, politically recognized and economically successful – or finding more chances for such success. Those who have more difficulty in fitting in tend to be excluded in a way or in another, depending on their group's size.

Regardless of whether one adapts well or not to the dominant ideology, repressing one's own psychology to fit in will always cause a negative psychological effect. These negative psychological effects are sometimes well noticeable and sometimes they are not. There are times such negative psychological aspects become the dominant ideology of a group, used by the group to assert their differentiation, as part of their group identity. But they seldom identify their ideology as being based on a repressed psychology rationalization.

An ideology, and its physiology, tend to see themselves as logic and rational while regarding alien ideologies (the ones they are apart) as irrational, stupid, inferior or mad. This is why many people in the past diagnosed with hysteria were sent to madhouses, especially women whose psychology tends to differ from Men's.

> "The game is played as if there is an objective reality
> that can be accurately perceived without implicating
> the perceiver"[2] (Siri Hustvedt, pag345)

Despite the fact that men can have, and normally have, some of the characteristics which are predominant in feminine psychology – and vice-versa – our society, that has a patriarchal materialist foundation, is based most on a masculine ideology and in a conservative society. With such ideological tradition, many women will have psychological distress caused by their own feminine psychology repression.

In postmodern societies, where women are largely emancipated, we find a combination of women well fitting to the dominant social psychology as well as society adaptation to some of the feminine psychology. We notice, for example, some strong masculine psychological behaviour, such as walking, talking and spontaneous reaction to distress, in societies like in Germany, as well as the

Nordic Countries, that is distinct from what we notice in Latin societies.

2

I said, at the beginning, that every society has many kinds of ideology in their psychology. Among them all there are two kinds of ideologies that I will give a generalized example based on my understanding so far. The first I like and the second I dislike because of my own physiology.

The first group is the kind who is often questioning things and, because of it, they are often questioning themselves. Consequently, they are more willing to listen to people and ponder about their positions. Even if they already have an opinion or belief about what the other person says they are willing to still find out if there is anything else to know, if something new will come up. Learn and perceive from the observation of the exterior world and not limiting the understanding of reality to the self [isolated rationalism]. So even when judging people they respect them. And even when certain about their own views and opinions they do not take things too seriously, because they know that eventually they might find out something else to learn about. In short, they are not absolutist – not religious – about what they have as their understanding, so they are able to adapt to changes and learn through unexpected casual circumstances which they set free.

This first group is often perceived as insecure by the second group and, in fact, when one questions too often one's own understanding insecurity tends to arise and becomes anxiety.

> "The things that fantasy can do is to normalize what
> psychologically is unbearable, thereby inuring us to it.
> In one case, fantasy beautifies the world. In the other,

it neutralizes it"[3] - (SONTAG, pag225)

The second group does not like to question their knowledge and beliefs because, for them, it is more important to have certainty; to be sure about one's own understanding and power than risking the uncertainty. For this reason, they are less willing to listen and ponder what people say because they do not like their certainty to be shaken. It causes them to have less respect towards different opinions, and they are less willing to adapt and learn things when changes come.

In other words, they are more conservatives. They are absolutists; if you propose another point of view they get offended. If pointed at problems in their absolutist rules it is not the rule that has problems but you for not fit in the rule, so finding problems in it.

It is ironic for the second group to perceive the first one as insecure because the second group is often highly insecure. For being insecure – insecure of changes, of losing the illusion of their power, of not knowing – they are attached to their certainties and are afraid of those who question what they have as absolutely true. They need it in order to feel confident and secure about themselves and, at the same time, they fear others' judgment about them if not shown they are right and certain about their beliefs.

On the other hand, the second group is more organized socially speaking, because their lack of questioning – what they have as absolute truth, moralistic and rules – makes them follow and fit in any rule and order regardless of what it is – regardless of circumstances. It means they are more bureaucratic and they also speak a more bureaucratic language – which denies options and, consequently, it denies responsibility. At the same time it results in them becoming less adaptable to what is not expected. When changes come they are the ones who have the more difficulty to adapt to the new reality, for being socially conservative, bureaucratic and absolutist.

The reason I like the first group is because individualism is more accepted among them. They allow people and themselves to be different (according to one's own psychology), accepting people as they are. Even if one looks and sounds weird for expressing a very distinctive personality. But while there is a sense of socio-psychological freedom in the first group it also has the side effects of a social crisis of belonging. Where there is pluralism and fast shifting of trends it is harder to find out where we belong to – especially in a society where you are supposed to conquer your identity (status or social recognition) through meritocracy. Such a crisis is less noticeable in the second group where people identify themselves in the social predominant psychology; an absolute order and behavior which they attempt to fit in regardless anything. But even then, the second group has its psychological side effects as well, which is well noticeable in their tendency to impatience, grumpiness, rage storming, social phobia and cynicism about whatever they don't identify themselves with. The alien ideologies and their psychologies that cause them to feel insecurities, for feeling it menacing their conformity, where they find their identity.

> "The most part we call "irrational" is just the Natural;
> but our "rationale" has become so unnatural that we
> see everything natural as irrational. Hence our
> psychology as the climax of men's self-realization is
> inadequate to explain change because it can only
> justify the type representing the existing social order
> of which it's an expression"[4] - (RANK).

Both groups can be part of any political spectrum. It doesn't make the person more left or more right wing in politics and economics if they are from either of the groups described.

1 RANK, O. *Psychology and The Soul*. Mansfield Centre: Martino Publishing, 2011

2 HUSTVEDT, S. "Borderlands: First, Second, and Third Person Adventures in Crossing Disciplines" in *A Woman Looking at Men Looking at Women: Essays on Art, Sex and the Mind*. UK: Sceptre,

3 SONTAG, S. "The Imagination of Disaster" in Against Interpretation. London: Pinguin Clasics, 2009

4 RANK, O. *Beyond Psychology*. New York: Dover, 1958.

THE MECHANICAL PHOTOGRAPHIC EYE CULTURE AND THE NEED OF ABSTRACT VISION

Photographers have a big outdoor culture. Most people interested in photography are usually also interested in outdoor activities, which they combine with photography, such as traveling, hiking, sports, nature, architecture, street photography and so on. No wonder that most photographers look for capturing experiences, especially now with social media' self-exposure.

Because of the fact photographs register the appearance of physical objects, in the real world, it was popularized by people wanting to register the tangibility of people and places they feel attached to, to keep as memory, as well as experiences that are related to such memories. But photography did not influence people on such tangibility registration alone. The publicity industry took a huge opportunity offered by photography – the image tangibility feeling and their tangible experiences – to induce people desiring the advertised object. Since images from publicity are everywhere we go, including in our homes through screens, we are all very much influenced by them, with our vision and feelings adapted to the language of tangibility in publicity language.

Such visual language is so influencing that most people, including most photographers, use such language as reference of quality in photography, with a lot of people trying to learn and copy the techniques of publicity to present it as skilled photographers.

The lock-down and social distancing caused by Coronavirus brought many photographers to share their innovative, creative and tutorials on how to practice photography without leaving home, as if photography indoor is something unusual. After all, most photographers are after new places out there in the world and new experiences in such places – expecting to obtain the new, the unusual or simply the distant experience. The good photos are often associated with how good a place looks like or how good the local experience is suggested to the viewer – The subject tangibility.

I feel the photography [visual] culture lost a lot along its materialist and technician path. Despite the artistic feeling of the activity it seems that most photographers lost – or are lacking – the most artistic thing one can have; the abstract vision.

> "What the greatest minds have ultimately sought from art is knowledge, a true and metaphysical knowledge, capable of reaching beyond the external appearance of phenomena in order to lead us to their intimate essence" [1]. – (Henry).

Many of the greatest photographers from the past did not have to go beyond their yards to find endless inspirations. Helmut Newton once said he could always find the perfect location and inspirations just around the corner. Georgio Morandi spent years painting nothing but bottles on plain background. But how can one find so many inspirations and be so prolific in a single place or even with a single kind of object and subject? The answer is Abstract vision. While most people only could see endless bottles in Morandi's paintings, he could see his hometown's rich landscape[2].

When we look beyond object appearance and tangibility we discover a new and wide world. With my still photographs I photographed the human feelings and vices using only bottles, food, candles and masks; pretty much the very same objects for hundreds of photographs, working only with light and composition to create new scenes, narratives and feelings. The same with self portrait works I did in a single corner in my apartment, using the same few objects and my body composition to create hundreds of expressions in photographs.

It seems the photography culture needs to rediscover still art photographs and return to a more abstraction vision, so photographers can discover they do not need to go far in order to find inspiration, to be prolific and to enjoy the most of the activity. It starts by enjoying one's own vision first, before looking into the camera viewfinder to find out how things look like from the camera mechanical point of view.

1 HENRY, M. *Seeing the Invisible on Kandinsky.* Continuum, 2009.

2 HUSTVEDT, S. "Georgio Morandi: Not Just Bottles" in HUSTVEDT, S. *Myteries Of The Rectangle: Essays on Painting.* Princeton Architectural Press; China, 2006

ART, LOVE, THE URGE TO APPEAR AND THE ANXIETY OF NONEXISTENCE

When we are born is when our existence starts. When we die is when we cease to exist. We appear and disappear. From the beginning of our existence we develop to the best of our appearance, then we deteriorate until we disappear.

As alive beings we react to what appears to us. Every smell, shape, colour, texture, and everything else that is perceived by the body, causes it to emote[1]. We may consciously or unconsciously notice our body emoting but, still, everything that appears to us tells us something about our own existence[2].

Because we perceive appearance we also want to appear.

> "Whatever can see wants to be seen, whatever can
> hear calls out to be heard, whatever can touch presents
> itself to be touched. It is indeed as though everything
> that is alive has the urge to appear, to fit itself in the
> world of appearances by displaying and showing, not
> its inner self but itself as an individual"
> (PORTMANN, 1967)[3]

As we perceive appearance and want to appear, our existence in this world presupposes a spectator[4]. Nothing that appears exists in the singular, it appears to something else who senses the other appearance; everything that is is meant to be perceived by somebody. Every subject is also an object. The appearance guarantees its objective reality[5].

Emoting, the body reaction to senses' stimulus as motion, is an automated body activity. Feeling is the nervous system reading of emotions and association of emotions to memories. As Antonio Damasio explains, emotions work in the field of the body while feelings work in the stage of the mind[6].

When something appears to our body, and we are conscious about our senses perception, it disappears to our mind. The contrary is also true; what comes to us as thoughts – mental pictures and words – ceases to exist as physical to our senses, even if the object in our mind is still in front of us[7]. Our mental pictures – our memories and feelings associated with them – keep the existence of images in the world of ideas, of what ceases to exist from our physical body perception. It is as if the physical world stops to exist when we are penetrated with thoughts. In the opposite direction, the experience of our body senses makes the mind silent and the object experienced with our senses feels real. Being capable to silence the mind, as in a meditative state, is to be willing to let go what temporarily appears to our body senses[8].

From shocking experiences of surprises, and fears, to great pleasures, the most impressive experiences are the ones that make us speechless, unable to describe, because our body and then our brain – which works constantly reading and interpreting our body emotions to generates feelings and memories[9] – are still processing the information; or because the object that appears to us is still very present to our body senses.

It is said that great works of art are the ones that make us speechless by silencing our mind, even though we always attempt to talk about them. Eventually, we turn away from the attention of our body emotion's experience and we drive our attention towards our mind – feelings and memories of the object we sensed the appearance of.

> The stimulation we call art characteristically requires
> us both to look very attentive and to look "beyond"
> what is understood as impediment, distraction,
> irrelevance [our thought]. (**SONTAG**, p.134)[10].

The great love experience is the one we perceive through our body – the body emotion intensity that drives our attention to it and quiets the mind – when we experience the best of the other person [the beloved one] existence; the height of their appearance to our senses. When the love experience is through the mind it only makes our body to emote to our imagination and memories expectation, instead of the real object or person. The very same is true when contemplating and experiencing art; both as creator and as spectator.

To have consciousness means to appear to oneself, but appearing to oneself – our mind – is not enough to guarantee its objective reality[11]; but only what appears to our body. *Only through the eye of another person the individual becomes an object to himself* (**HUSTVEDT**, p.370)[12]. Through artistic expression, such as painting, writing, sculpture and photography, we are always communicating to somebody, a spectator, to whom we want to appear; even if the spectators is one's own self; The individual self narrative – where is formed the person's sense of identity[13]. It is as if the urge to create is a desire to appear in another object through which our existence can be perceived beyond ourselves. The artistic work is also where artists appear to themselves, this time not only through the self narrative of the mind but through a materialized self to be experienced by virtue of their bodies' senses – emotions – in the objective world; as the confirmation of their existence to themselves.

The same is the people's reaction to our own appearance, which confirms to us our own existence. When such interaction is lacking we feel invisible. Thus, the body feels hungry to confirm its existence; it feels empty. It feels as if we are disappearing, resulting in anxiety and apprehensiveness about a lack of a perceiving self existence, which can only feels rested again once the senses are fed with the interactive reaction of its appearance to another person, confirming, then, its existence.

In such perspective, the dream which we always have when sleeping, regardless of our memory of them when we are awake, is a mental stimulation to the emotion of our body, to confirm its existence; A mental self assurance to confirm the body is still reacting, still alive[14].

The anxiety to create something beyond our own, where we appear in, to guarantee our appearance and self perpetuation through, comes from the awareness of our own death, which is the great anxiety one can have as a human. We fear our disappearance. Because of such fear we create culture, traditions, societies, family, mythologies, religions and, along it all, art[15].

The common scientific sense, which is highly materialistic, understands appearance as a function to the body preservation and survival. What if our complex body function is what works for our appearance sake?

Despite the mind, the body has its own impulses, its own automated behavior, its emotion. Even mono-cellular and protocell life reacts to what appears to them, as a bodily impulse. It is what Spinoza called Conatus; the power of existence[16]. What ancient tribal cultures in the far east called Mana; the energy which everything appears from[17]. To be, is to possess desires. Homeostasis is what defines life, the impulse [desire] to preserve, perpetuate itself and guarantee its existence, self-confirming through its self-display.

[1, 6, 9] DAMASIO, A. *The strange order of things: Life, feeling, and the making of cultures.* New York: Vintage Books, 2019.

[2] EDEL, L. *Henry James:* A life. New York: Harper & Row, 1985.

[4, 9] HUSTVEDT, S. "My Louise Bourgeois". In; HUSTVEDT, S. *A Woman Looking at Men Looking at Women: Esseys on Art, Sex, and the Mind.* UK: Sceptre, 2016.

[3, 5, 7, 11] ARENDT, H. *The Life of the Mind: The groundbreaking investigation on how we think.* New York: Houghton Mifflin Harcourt, 1977.

[8] WATTS, A. *Tao: The Watercourse Way.* New York: Pantheon Books, 1975.

[10] SONTAG, S. "A Note on Bunraku" in *Where the Stress Falls.* England: Pinguin Books, 2009.

[12] HUSTVEDT, S. "Embodied Vision: What Does It Means to Look at a Work of Art?" in *Living, Thinking, Looking.* England: Sceptre, 2013

[13] SACKS, O. "The Lost Mariner" in *The Man Who Mistook His Wife for a Hat.* London: Picador, 2011.

[14, 15, 17] RANK, O. *Psychology and The Soul.* Mansfield Center, CT : Martino Publishing, 2011.

[16] SPINOZA, B. *Spinoza Reader: The "Ethics" and Other Work.* Princeton: Princeton University Press, 1994.

Capitalism and Social Alienation

1

It is known and unanimously understood by all economic schools, political strands and social science, that because of its accelerated economic growth through credit – which is just another name for debt – for the competition and betting in the future demands, capitalism eventually creates an over production that exceeds the demand; which means crises, because the exceeded offer causes prices to plunge under the production and profits level, making business not able to recover their investments[1].

Keynesian economic policies were introduced after the big economic crisis of 1929, and the Second World War, as an attempt to delay as long as possible the next crisis, by using the governmental purchasing power to create demand and rise prices in the competitive level again; So business can keep working, having profits and hiring workers. But Keynes' economic theory does not offer a definitive solution to crises, since overproduction and over accumulation crises can only be solved by destruction of the exceeded offer[2]. Governmental investments will spare the economy and its people from crises but only for a while because, while business are having profits, competitive capitalism will keep increasing and accelerate productivity – as attempt to reduce production costs, compete against other business with prices, with the goal of always have bigger profits and stability in the market by dominating it – until eventual flood of exceeded production in the markt[3].

Keynesian theory came in the early 20th century but its practice is much older than that. One of the best known examples among many was during the Louis Napoleon Regime, which invested heavily in the modernization of Paris, in the second half of 19th century, in order to prevent the French economy from entering into crisis[4]. But since the crisis can not be delayed forever governments have been trying many other alternative practices to deal with the production (and money) over accumulation, such as finding more demand abroad and wars, because wars naturally cause destruction and demand investments so creating new demands from market production. This is the reason European countries had so many wars among each other during modernity[5], they were fighting to open each other's market to send their production. This is also the reason countries practice protectionism and the reason trade wars lead to military wars. In short, because capitalism creates overproduction – of goods, services and money, which causes them to lose value – capitalism is constantly growing. If anything stops its growth, such as a limited market, limited money, borders and so on, it enters into stagnation or crisis. So capitalism is always looking for new and bigger markets to grow, which often means in other countries. When capitalism does not find it, governments enter in shock against each other to protect their own markets from each other.

Europe Union and other economic blocks came as a solution to avoid conflicts among their countries and unite their markets for a bigger geopolitical influence globally, such as the economic dumping the European Union practice in African countries; Which they promote as a positive free market for sending their overproduction and cheap price products to poor countries. What is actually happening is the export of crises[6]; African and other poor countries worldwide are being dumped with products, causing local businesses not being able to compete in their markets with flooded production.

Many people in developed countries complain about the immigrants "stealing their jobs" or accusing them for causing the drop in the wages because of excess labor work offered in the market. These people seem not to realize that developed countries stole the immigrants' jobs first. Because countries like Germany and the United States have huge production subsided by the government in order to keep business producing and hiring workers artificially – not because of market demands[7]. This is why milk, pork, fruits and many other products are so cheap. German farmers don't have any profit with the prices of milk and pork that are sold in supermarkets, so the government keeps paying producers to not stop producing and not stop hiring workers. Germany, then, through the European Union, dumps the over production in African countries in order to avoid further drop in prices, and so in order to avoid spending more money in subsidies. The industrialized subsidized products, made of subsidized milk and pork in Europe, floods poor countries markets, where local businesses can not compete with subsidized European products (which are literally free), so local businesses have no profits ending up with closed doors. Workers without jobs and low wage in poor countries migrate to countries where there are more opportunities to find jobs and higher wages, such as the subsidized European market. This is the export crisis Europe and the US practice in poor countries.

China has been dumping their dirty cheap production all over the world. On the other hand, it also has been practicing a massive Keynesianism by building cities, roads, and all kinds of structures, as well as industrial subsidies not only in China but worldwide. China can do it because it has a huge capital reserve. It is also the reason China was buying a huge amount of commodities from all over the world, which saved not only China but the entire planet from a worse crisis after 2008. It was the reason developing countries were booming selling huge amounts of commodities to China. But once China's economy slowed down not only the developing countries went into economic crisis but also the developed countries such as Germany and the US felt the impact.

The later 1970's and the 1980's were characterized by the end of Keynesian economic policy and the weakening of social democracy politics in developed countries; Instead of using the government purchasing power – to create demand and cause a delay of the crisis – it was decided to face crises and practice austerity. But the changes for austerity were only for the population – for society – not for big business. As far as corporations can keep accumulating wealth it doesn't matter for them if society is in crisis, so the focus became the speculative market where big business always can invest money when over accumulated, to keep the value up, and buy up when the market is in crisis, instead of invest in society. This is why statistics show that the economy is booming when big businesses are making profits despite the impoverishment of the population. Their solution was the guarantee of the stability of those with wealth, since capitalism can not guarantee stability for all. But once such a decision is made it nullifies what capitalism was supposed to be (so people say), a competition; Once a group or economic class has stability it is not competing. This is the biggest capitalism contradiction because it is supposed to be about competition, but every competitor in a game is looking to win the game by eliminating their competitors – to become unable to be competed against – and when it happens the game is over.

When western industries migrated to the cheaper production costs in China, western countries started deindustrializing and along with this change – which caused the weakening of labor unions and left wing parties[8] – unemployment rose and wages stagnated, causing the losing of workers rights and temporary or mini jobs increase, resulting in a big population of working-poor in countries like the US, UK and Germany. This situation created a socioeconomic insecurity in the population leading to populist political influences and political extremists gaining numbers in the political arena. What also happened was the middle class becoming more supportive of the minorities courses, since the bigger social gap between rich and poor approaches the middle class, now poorer, to the working class. Thus racism and political violence, which has always been a problem, emerges in the mainstream political fight today – among many other political causes in support of the so-called minorities (the economically and socially excluded).

Many people complain that big businesses have been increasing profits while workers's wage has not accompanied business productivity growth. It is as if we do not know that capitalism never meant to pay workers for their labor productivity, reason why workers are paid by working time – which literally makes workers' labor become cheaper the more productive they are. The labor productivity gain is for capitalists to keep as their profits, as return to their business investment, which is what the socialist and communists movements fight against, since productivity investments are only possible because of their labor.

The fact is, insecurity creates many expectations for people who hope, through their effort and own means, to overcome something they fear. When the person doesn't archive what they hoped for, the individual improvement they were expecting, or what they want to maintain – maintain their jobs, maintain their wages, maintain their homes, maintain their routines or just maintain their confidence – they become frustrated, and from frustration comes hate.

2

Every feeling is a somatic experience. Whatever we feel is the mental state created by our body condition – muscles stress, heartbeat, body temperature, etc. We have many names for what we feel but only because we know the context which created the feeling. Often, all the different feelings come from the same somatic state of instability – with its diverse levels. Frustration is the feeling a person has of hating the self, for being unhappy with the expectation not obtained to the self, or fearing not having the acting power to archive what they desire; It is a somatic irritation or discomfort for feeling powerless. When an individual loses hopes in their own acting power they tend to give up further expectations, as a way to avoid further frustration of acting in it. In such mental perspective the person tends to have his attention towards his past experiences; The less we have for the *Will* to act – the somatic experience in the material world – the more we tend to spend our time thinking; Experiencing life in our minds – often to withdraw from reality for feeling powerless in it (and feeling excluded from society where one feels belonging only through their acting in it) – and the excess of thinking leads to depression.

The frustration can have another shape though. In order to protect oneself from self-hate, the person tends to project their hate onto the external world, where they will find a target which they will tend to blame for their frustration. The external projected hate becomes a target to be destroyed. The target is transformed into an enemy which the destruction becomes a symbol of overcoming their frustration[9]. This is the setting which brings populism to the political stage; The promise of a hero who has the supposing acting power to destroy an enemy, which symbolizes a group's frustration.

Every act of frustration – and so hate that tends to be projected on something external from the self as protection from, or react to, self-hate – tends to the wish and act of destruction. The destruction is not only a hope to destroy the frustration projected on something in the material world but it is, before anything else, a hope that from the destruction, and chaos it creates, somebody with a power of acting will appear to put an order that will ease the person's frustration (powerless feeling). Frustration is the feeling of internal chaos, together with the feeling of not having power to act and to put an order in the emotional chaos. Insecurity, then, is the feeling of not trusting their own acting power and so feeling weak, for not being able to guarantee the realization of an expectation.

Populists leaders use the masses insecurity and hate, by helping them in creating an enemy to become their target, in order to obtain public support in their political and economical agenda, and one of these agendas is Fascism.

3

When people talk about fascism they talk about their political propaganda and mythologies; not what it really is or its goal. Its roots date back from the end of the Medieval economic system, where artisans and craftsmen's markets were protected by guilds that guaranteed their social and economic stability[10]. The same for land owners who had their social and economic stability guaranteed by their land and their private army. Even peasants had the security of the land where they belonged. Wherever social position the person was born in they would tend to remain in that position for all their lives, as did their ancestors, as if it was their divine nature, or their blood and family natural rights and natural fate. Capitalism made it possible for people to climb the socioeconomic ladder through trade. The rise of steam industries attracted many traders who would transport the goods from producers to consumers. National States with their governmental army could protect the territory, private lands and contracts for industries, traders and customers to have the safety to do business. A family could own land without the need of a private army to protect it and without the worry of losing their land and goods to someone else's private army. It was in this change – from a no competitive society to a competitive one, to climb the social ladder, to make as much money as possible, to fight for the bigger market by beating their competitors, all in order to guarantee their socioeconomic stability against their competitors – that many people started claiming their supposed natural rights to land, to money, to social position, seeking more stability for their socioeconomic permanence, against the capitalist and central government economy that led the middle class (the artisans in the medieval system) living in the constant risk of becoming working class, or obtaining piles of debts in order to compete in capitalism. Peasants kicked out of the land became forced to sell their labor to employers, becoming dependable of their employers' businesses stability. This is where the pan-european movement came from. Campaigns to return to the stability for the medieval system was propagated by the old land owners and had much support from the middle class. In an attempt to stop people from supporting the return of the old system, governments implemented politics of market protection, blocking the borders from foreign businesses and foreign workers, implementing welfare systems and using their political power and army to gain foreign markets, all to give people – especially the petite bourgeoisie and farmers (the middle class) – the guarantee of a minimum socioeconomic safety against free market competition instability. This is the root of Nationalism and other things fascism fights for.

Fascism aims to limit competition among social classes, making it harder or impossible for the working class to compete with middle class and capitalists, as well as making it harder for the middle class to compete with the upper class for their socioeconomic position, by plastering social classes to guarantee social stability to the middle and upper class. The reason Mussolini's Fascism also gives strong rights to workers, for them to become more pleased with their social position and less willing to compete among other social classes with the attempt of climbing the social ladder, for better life condition and stability in life.

The rise of fascist tendency, with the right wing extremists gaining political attention among the population, specially the middle class, is because they feel a socioeconomic insecurity in this political austere and so-called free market – which is not really free, since today's governments work in taking financial risks in the name of big business, to protect them from risks by speculate in the debt markets, in eugenic constructions as well as sports and tourism events, for example, in order to attract big businesses, and, if it works it last not enough to recover the government speculation, that uses taxpayers' money to guarantee big businesses profits.

The reason fascists, Nazis, the KKK, claim to have natural superiority, and so natural rights, above other people, is because they need such ideals about themselves in order to hide – first from themselves and then from others – their insecurity about themselves, created by social and economic changes. Thus, the frustration of feeling individually powerless in their act to overcome their insecurity. The fear of others – minorities – taking their social and economic position in society, and so the fear of not being able to compete against them in order to avoid poverty, financial debt or the fear to become the victims of their own prejudices against minorities.

As an attempt to overcome their frustration – which means self-hate for feeling powerless in their individual act – they create the imaginary and mythological idea of their natural superiority and natural rights, in order to have a reason to gain self-love again, and so project their hate to a target outside of their own which they will blame as the reason of their frustration. For this reason, they attempt to fight against the target and destroy it as a symbolism of the destruction of the chaotic feeling they have in themselves, that generates their frustration.

Nothing this is new. It is the reason for Christianity to come, promising the guarantee of a natural eternal safety in an afterlife paradise, for all, against all mundane odds – through Agape love; The love for God through people and the love for people through God, unconditionally. Through such christian love one becomes able to recognize themselves through other people, thus being able to love the self where they find God. In other words, It is to find God inside yourself through empathy and consequently you will find god in people as well. It is a strategy to avoid feeling alienated from people, and so not feeling threatened by them. But much of it is lost through the competitive materialist society that puts people against each other for their own individualist interest, which creates social phobia.

For this reason, I don't believe we can fight hate or any popular and political movement based on hate. Fighting hate seems only to lead to more frustration and more hate. Instead, I think there is only one way to fight hate and it is through the creation of socioeconomic stability; but, not through segregation and alienation of people from each other. This is the biggest challenge in a society that only found a way to create and accumulate fast and huge wealth through self-interest and competitive instability.

4

There is a fundamental process in the use of our senses that is the confirmation of ourselves through the interaction with other people and information that we capture. Because everything we have contact with causes a somatic reaction, which when analyzed by our brain and transformed into feeling it says something about ourselves to ourselves. Therefore, we are after information, in general, not for knowledge but for certainty; Knowledge demands doubts and questioning while certainty does not. We want certainty to confirm to ourselves about who we are and where we belong to, or, at least, to convince ourselves about the beliefs we want have about ourselves; The biggest emotional pain one can have is the uncertainty about who one is and where one belongs to[11]; The place, people and tradition in which people perpetuate themselves in their act[12]. Our mind was not made to understand reality and the world beyond our reality, it was made to guarantee our existence (quick adaptation for our self-preservation and self-perpetuation)[13].

For very long, people believed that before agriculture humans were miserable for constant living in starvation and fear. Only in the middle of 20th century, through archaeological findings, researchers found out that humans had a much happier and healthier life before agriculture, for having better and richer food varieties, plenty of free time and the pleasure of their exploring instinct. What we call evolution is actually leading us to the so-called evolution trap, because we convince ourselves about becoming more happy when in fact we are becoming more miserable. Happiness is not a state of being, it is not what remains, it is felt in changes; the achievement of our act. We have achieved a lot with our acts to make us feel happy, but such acts are mostly to overcome the miserable conditions that we created in today's society and that we can not be completely free from.

1 DALIO, R. *How the Economic Machine Works*. http://www.economicprinciples.org.

2 HARVEY, D. "The Geography of Capitalist Accumulation: A Reconstruction of The Marxian Theory" in *The Ways Of The World*. London: Profile Books, 2017

3 HARVEY, D. *Marx, Capital And The Madness Of Economic Reason.* London: Profile Books, 2019

4 HARVEY, D. "Introduction" in *The Ways Of The World.* London: Profile Books, 2017 (pag. 2)

5 MARX, K. *The Eighteenth Brumaire of Louis Napoleon.* Wiscosin: Wiseblood, 2013

6 HICKEL, J. "The Development Delusion: Foreign Aid and Inequality" in *American Affairs.* Volume I, Number 3, Fall 2017.

7 ACHTNICH, T. *Game of No Rules: The deceptive promise of free trade.* Germany: Südwestrundfunk, 2018

8 MITCHELL, W and FAZI, T "Make The Left Great Again" in *American Affairs*. Volume I, Number 3, Fall 2017.

9 WINNICOTT, D. *Human Nature.* London: Free Association Books, 1999.

10 ARENDT, H. *Origins of Totalitarianism.* UK: Pinguin Classics, 2017.

11 REINCH II, R. M. "The Burdens of Belonging" in *American Affairs.* Volume I, Number 3, Fall 2017.

12 RANK, O. *Psychology and The Soul.* Mansfield Center, CT : Martino Publishing, 2011.

13 DAMASIO, A. *The strange order of things: Life, feeling, and the making of cultures.* New York: Vintage Books, 2019.

PLAYING ALONE

1

We can estimate but never predict the future. We never know what changes in the wind may occur once we throw the arrow of our action. For this reason we never know exactly how our lives will be once we put our planning in action. The target, then, works only as inspiration, orientation and reference. To act is always a risk taking. When traveling to Israel I thought my experience there would be of hard and boring work, and it was, but many unexpected experiences came along and left their stamps in my memory, which make me forget about the boring and hard moments as irrelevant. My negative expectation may have caused me to appreciate the good experiences much better, reason why positive expectations can be dangerous, by making the person not appreciate the positive aspects of their experiences because of higher goals. Negative expectations can be even more dangerous, because we think we are happy for what we got since it is more than we expected, accepting what actually may still make us miserable, for believing to be in an advantage or privileged position, not willing to risk losing it with further action. Similar to when I talk about the health care in Germany as not being public, not being universal and not being free but the contrary; it is mostly private and very expensive – different from what people abroad believe and say. Also different from what a lot of Germans tell foreigners or themselves. When presented to such questioning the answer is often a comparison to other countries – specially comparison to American health care system, not because it is good but, the opposite, because any other system looks good compared to America's – in order to point what they got as better than what they are comparing it to, so to accept what they got as it is, as justification to not take the risk inherent in action to change it, overlooking its own reality.

We look for happiness and pleasures in life. Different from what many people think, happiness and pleasure are not sensed in a constant state of mind, body and life. It is found in changes, in the overcoming of distress. They are the transitional state of mind. *"It is action, not rest, that constitutes our pleasure"* (John Adams). This is what games do for us, they present us distress to overcome, to sense pleasure out of the challenging stress. The game or the entertainment are safe spaces to risk action for not belonging to and not affecting our real lives – unless we bring our real lives to them or them to our real lives – so they can be a distraction from the challenges of real life, as a way to accept what we got in real life, for having somewhere else to risk action and whatever else to pursue pleasures.

We all have the impulses to act and from our act to create something. These things that we create is the materialization in the world of what is in our mind. The mind which is what Antonio Damasio demonstrates to be created by our emotion and feelings (somatic experiences)[1]. The risk of not having control of the outcome of our action[2] is the reason that in tragedies the hero tends to die, or suffer at the end of his life[3]. The hero's mythological narrative is the expression of a fear, of what we today call *Will Power.* The hero is the person with a strong *Will* to act in life, but who also suffers the consequences of the unpredictability of his act.

Every *Will* to act comes with the opposite force in us which blocks us to act, because of fear. The fear of losing control of our act or its unexpected outcome[4]. This fear is unconscious but it is where our taboos, empathies and social rules come from. People who lack it act beyond moral, ethical, empathical or social norms, willing to risk everything in their action without fear, because they have no sense of having a self (to lose); They are psychopaths[5].

2

Otto Rank described three types of individuals. The first is the so-called normal people, which is what society judges to be the people who fit in and adapt well to society's psychological ideology. The so-called normal people, according to Rank, are the ones who can well balance their act and their fears. They can do that because they feel *being part of the total* in society; Their act, work, creation, contributing in a small proportion to their families, communities, societies and jobs, makes them feel integrated to it all, and so feel fulfilled. It requires no much impulse to act, or *Will*, to feel fulfilled from their act – and so having a sense belonging[6].

The neurotics are the second type described by Rank – using the term from the past, which among others are what we call the anxious people nowadays. They are the people who have a psychology that do not fit in the dominant psychological ideology. They have trouble adapting or changing their psychology in order to fit in. For society, and its modern and postmodern ideology standard, they have psychological problems that must be fixed, because any psychology that does not fit in the modern and postmodern economic demands is seen as illness. What Otto Rank, and many other thinkers from the past, suggested is that neurotic people have no psychological problem at all; no illness. Their problem, instead, is society which excludes them. Their illness is caused by society forcing them to repress who they are in order to fit them in society's limited standards. This limitation was narrowed with the capitalist work doctrine and the equality ideology. The neurotic agony is for feeling segregated and alienated from society, because it is how society sees and treats them. Because of their segregated feeling, different from the so-called normal people, neurotics have a strong desire to act as an attempt to fit in, to "become normal", and with their action a hope to feel belonging to it[7]. Such strong impulse to plunge in life and act in it creates an equal very strong fear, making them unable to act[8]. They find themselves blocked in their fear and, consequently, they feel being aside from society; The society which demands the neurotics to fit in and be "normal"; not "lazy".

Artists are like the Neurotics. Artists also have a very strong impulse to act, also because of feeling segregated from the world as it is. But artists accept to not belong to society and they deliberately want to be aside from society, because they found a way to be who they are in their own isolated world, where they find the pleasure of their act, as overcoming the distress from society by creating their own world. What differs artists type from neurotics is that the first can eventually find a balance between being who they are and acting in the world as it is. After having the pleasure of acting in their own isolated world, with their art where they can be who they are, artists are able to step in and act in the social world as it is; After creating his art the artist feels fulfilled and so they are able to step in the world of the average humans to act in it, until the impulse that makes them to feel segregated from it kicks in again, making them step out of society and isolate themselves in their creative world[9].

Neurotics do not accept their feelings of not belonging and so they do not accept to be segregated, different or aside from society's psychological ideology standard. Their strong will to act, and fear that blocks them to act, is because they desperately want to recreate themselves, attempting to fit in society. While artists embrace who they are, not only accepting their identity and being apart from society as it is, they want to go beyond by stamping their psychology and individual identity in their creative act; acting against society that wants to make them "normal".

It seems to me that the artist type, because they can step in and out of the common world of men and women – as somebody who can step out of a landscape and so see its total – is able to understand and see certain aspects of life that average people are not able to see so clearly. They can see the stage where people interact with each other, but as spectators and not only as actors.

3

The classic understanding of hypocrite is of a person who is not lying to others but to themselves; Because hypocrites are, before anyone else, lying to themselves they are being sincere to people who they express the beliefs they have convinced themselves of[10]. In this classic understanding we, in a certain way, are all hypocrites because we all have two sides; the individual side which acts in private and the social side which acts in public. After a certain age in our childhood we start to act another self, other than our own, in order to have privacy for our individual self, to not over expose ourselves, afraid of being alienated from the social because of our individuality, so we can feel we fit in[11]. Before we become able to act and learn to act in society during our childhood – when we feel over exposed and vulnerable in the social arena – we cry of frustration for being lost and not knowing what to do. When a mother of a 3 years old child told her daughter to say "hello" to me the little girl hesitated for a couple of seconds before starting crying, confused by her mother's demands and lost in how to act; for feeling frustrated in her new and unfamiliar experience. One of the main functions of playing during childhood is the learning of acting. Pretending situations in order to gain familiarity with them. Pretending to be something or someone else; thus hide the individual self. Eventually, we become so used to our act that we mistake ourselves with the idealized character we act in public, until we become unaware of our acting and others acting in the stage of social life.

4

This acting in the social stage of life is what makes us social beings, which the classic philosophers called *political beings*[12]. Society is an artificial arena we create for ourselves, so in it we can be equals; since originally and essentially we are not equals but different and unique[13]. What makes people equal is the public realm of politics.

> "Isonomy guaranteed equality, but not because all men
> were born or created equal, but, on the contrary,
> because men were by nature not equal, and needed an
> artificial institution, the polis, which by virtue of its
> space would make them equal" (Hannah Arendt).

Equality exists only in this specifically political realm, where men and women meet one another as citizens and not as *private* persons. The equality of the Polis was an attribute of the Polis and not of people, who received their equality by virtue of citizenship and not by virtue of birth. Neither equality or freedom was understood as a quality inherent in human nature. They were the artificial human effort and qualities of a man-made world[14].

This public political appearance – the act under people's eyes –

is what makes humans civilized. Without it (without feeling equal) there is no politics but violence; where humans become beasts. This is why medieval Christian philosophers wrote that God's ubiquitousness is because he is in the eyes of every person – and so in every person. The reason Christianity main philosophy is Agape: Find God in people and people in God, thus people can love each other unconditionally. This love gives two individuals the trust to act with each other, hence feeling fulfilled in their act together[15]. Without such love one feels alienated from people, therefore feeling threatened by them, incapable to act with each other which causes anxieties.

5

The first thing I noticed when I moved to Germany was that Germans have social anxieties – and I would say that Brazilian, who are very social, also have strong social anxieties but of a different kind. Before Germany I was living in Ireland, where talking with strangers in any situation is common and even the opposite of what I experience in Germany; Instead of anxiety the Irish feel comforted when interacting with another person. What differs the Irish from the German is that the first have a more ludic approach to life, to their act, while Germans take it as a serious matter; averse to risk and so averse to act.

Every apartment and houses I have lived in Germany has problems with the walls, causing one to hear clearly what happens on the other side as if there is no wall at all. While it is said that privacy is an important thing for Germans I feel I never had privacy in Germany; I can hear every private talk and intimate life of my neighbours, and they can hear mine. It makes me feel I am never on my own, and everything I do I have to be concerned about those who may hear it – One feels lonely when in a companion of people they can not interact with and expose themselves; not when alone. For that reason I gave up playing guitar, I gave up still photography at home and I gave up some workouts at home just to respect my neighbours' space; to not distract them with my presence. What was left for me was reading books, practicing yoga, listening to music and movies with headphones. On the other hand, reading and Yoga is also difficult because three of my neighbours do not have the same care, which makes it hard to do anything that demands a certain concentration.

Eventually I developed Tonic Tensor Tympani Syndrome – which is caused when one over protects or over stimulates their ears – as I was always wearing earplugs or headphones at home. My problem doubled then, because while I can not leave home or open the windows without protecting my over sensitive ears, caused by the syndrome, I have now to avoid wearing earplugs as much as possible at home in order to not make it worse.

I tried to talk to the loud neighbours but they didn't help. I talked to the building administrator but he also didn't care, nor the police. What they all say is that the building is old and there is nothing they can do about it. It sounds as denying to actually face the problem, by accepting it, and pretending the problem is not social but individual; Me, who as a complaining person does not fit in and wants to act. But it is exactly for the building being old and having problems people should be extra careful, not careless pretending that there are no problems by just accepting them. I was even told to not go talk to my upstairs neighbour for him being very old. They expect me to not talk to a neighbour about him being loud, meanwhile I developed an illness and nobody cares about helping me to get better but worse; Because I am young I am expected to be "strong". I sure would move out if I had the financial conditions. The point is the social norm, created to avoid individual action and individual standing out, contrasting against the egalitarian social ideology – conformity.

This lack of privacy makes it difficult to be alone with one's own thoughts, which is essential for the psychological aspect of the individual being; Being able to step outside of the social stage and have a private life for the private self[16].

> "Never is he more active than when he does nothing,
> never is he less alone than when he is by himself."
> (Cato)

With my ears' condition I could not work in the job I had and I should not work on most jobs. From a successful self-employed business I became jobless, so I had got a part-time job in order to have money. Because it is hard to sleep with loud neighbours, when I should not wear earplugs, I had missed many days of work because of tiredness, which makes it hard to keep any job I may get. So I got fired from the job I had got.

I talked to my quiet neighbours and they told me that they do not complain about the loud people because they feel scared or because they know it will not help. One of them suggested I put on loud music and hope for the loud neighbours to move out. Apparently, it is what some people feel as the only acting option; the violence.

What calls my attention is the fact that people avoid talking to their neighbours. When I try they behave annoyed and anxious to end the talk, or in denial of the loudness despite it being evident. In short, people feel very alienated from each other. When people feel alienated there is no politics because politics is the safe space where people can talk – and then act – with each other as equals; Where empathy emerges because it means to find oneself in others' shoes. As the ancient Greek philosophers said, we are political beings because we are able to talk, which requires interaction with another human being. Without it, without the political space where we can find ourselves in one another, what remains is violence; This violence is often expressed in absolutist certitude, used as a tool to avoid the need to understand people and situations[17]; Reducing reality to a miserable standard.

While in Germany – and in many countries worldwide – it is common for people to show certainty about everything, what it hides is the fear of being wrong, of having no power, of the uncertainty of action's outcome; The strong certainty is the social *Self* hiding the individual *Self*'s fears, and denying such fears to themselves and then to those who they act with. Which is what I believe to be what makes Germans anxious. Their attempt of perfectionism requires a technocratic absolutist certitude, so people's unpredictable individualism and particularities are obstacles to it. While one can persuade themselves of knowing and thus solving everything, what actually happens is people resuming reality to standardized rules that make sense to their certainties, not to reality itself. They avoid adventure in the unknown outcome of spontaneous act[18], for being afraid of it – of being spontaneous.

I went to several doctors looking for help with my Tonic Tensor Tympani Syndrome. Instead of investigating it they tell me it is just Tinnitus and nothing else. They ignore my pains and complaints as if I am giving excuses, for being lazy, for not wanting to work or for being dramatic. Because doctors ignore my complaints and pretend there is nothing wrong my illness only gets worse. So I did what doctors hate the most, I tried to find out about my condition on the internet and I got a rich didactic information, therapy and prevention that doctors I visited never gave me.

I always thought of doctors as problem solvers, which does not mean they solve all illnesses and complications but investigate them with the attempt to understand and solve them. It is not the experience I have had so far. This problem is not particular to

Germany, but Germany has a bureaucratic approach to life. When a doctor told me to avoid loud places I asked her to write it down, so I could present it to my boss and to JobCenter. She said she could not do it because, according to her, what I have is just Tinnitus. For the bureaucratic system, which includes the health system, I am not ill, despite my complaints.

> "My senior for tomorrow told me `I expect you to be
> 0% knowledgeable but 100% reliable.` I've been
> repeating it to myself all day. THAT I can deliver.."
> (@Scrublifemd on Twitter).

And this kind of denial of problems, pretending everything is just doing fine – showing a big certainty and being annoyed with any kind of questioning of their "know better" – is the norm. As the very common scene of people smoking on door passages; While they are technically outside the smoke comes inside of the building, and everybody just pretends all is fine because they are technically following the rules, which becomes an useless rule then. A lot of people get angry or annoyed if asked to smoke somewhere else; Ask to adapt themselves to the situation and individuals around them, which the rules were supposed to be working for.

The strong attachment to rules seems a way of being able to live in society without concerns about people, in obliviousness, without the need to adapt to each situation, so avoiding interaction with strangers; avoid politics. Instead of adapting to individual's situations, with individual decision and action – which requires spontaneity – they rely on the violence of bureaucratic rules that maintains people alienated from each other. A bureaucratic social relation and communication, because bureaucracy is impersonal; It is not the individual's act choice but the violent imposed rule from a power above. From this psychological point of view people feel they have no responsibility for their acts, and so they feel they have no responsibilities for the consequence of their act on people around them; They lack the sense of guilt.

6

Everywhere else, as contrast, we have the motivational ideology preaching that everything has a solution. But solutions are not for the public helm because problems are privatized[19]. Thus, the individual has to deal with social problems they find themselves in as their individual problems, accepting social problems as *just life as it is*. The solution may not be legal, moral or ethical when one believes that there is no individual problem that one can not overcome on their own, with the stigma of being seen as lazy or maladjusted if they don't. If there were no problems without a solution one can solve on their own we would be God itself; which seems to be what many people are attempting to become but they become evil instead, for becoming over certain of their individual act.

Today, we do not believe in finding God in others – as the Christian love (Agape) once thought people – but solely in us, as individuals and not as social beings, which is basically the same as believing to be God itself.

In a world where you are seen as lazy if you do not overcome all your obstacles a lot of people are left behind, seen as deserving their fate or as victims of *reality as it is*. Hoping for bureaucratic public institutions to take care of everybody, so people do not have to act spontaneously to one another. It makes a society of lonely isolated people[20], even when one finds no real privacy to step out of the public stage.

People try to show their support and help without actually

understanding people but by giving generic advice, which is just pretending they are helping people – by convincing themselves of being helpful to others. Without trying to understand the individual particularities and spontaneous act of those they want to help – so to help them in their particularities – there is no real help. It makes people, who are supposed to get help and support, feel even more isolated. People who are anxious, depressed, isolated and feeling left behind do not need generic advice but social integration[21]; Being able to step in to act in public as they are, and step out to live their private inner world. Otherwise they feel locked in their private inner world; not being able to act in the stage of life, at the same time not knowing their individual self which is found through playing and interacting with people. The biggest and main, if not only, help they need is to be understood, is to have people who listen to them, is to be able to act; play in the stage of life and take it as it really is: just a play, where we can materialize our inner world by expressing our feelings, which are our somatic experiences.

> "The poor man's conscience is clear; yet he is
> ashamed.[...] He feels himself out of the sight of
> others, groping in the dark. [...] He is not disapproved,
> censured, or reproached; he is only not seen. [...] To be
> wholly overlooked, and to know it, are intolerable."
> (John Adams).

[1] DAMASIO, A. *The strange order of things: Life, feeling, and the making of cultures.* New York: Vintage Books, 2019.

[2, 13] ARENDT, H. *The Human Condition.* Chicago: University of Chicago Press, 2018.

Second Edition.

[3, 4, 5, 18] RANK, O. *Psychology and The Soul.* Mansfield Center, CT : Martino Publishing, 2011.

[4, 8, 15, 16] ARENDT, H. *The Life of the Mind: The groundbreaking investigation on how we think.* New York: Houghton Mifflin Harcourt, 1977.

[6, 7, 9] RANK, O. *Art and Artists: Creative Urge and Personality Development.* New York: W.W. Norton, 1989.

[10,12,13, 14] ARENDT, H. *On Revolution.* London: Faber & Faber, 2016.

[11] WINNICOTT, D.W. *Human Nature.* London: Free Association Books, 1999.

[17, 18, 20] RANK, O. *Beyond Psychology.* New York: Dover, 1958.

[19] ARENDT, H. *Origins of Totalitarianism.* UK: Pinguin Classics, 2017.

[21] HUSTVEDT, S. "The Writing Self and the Psychiatric Patient" in *A Woman Looking at Men Looking at Women: Essays on Art, Sex and the Mind.* UK: Sceptre, 2017.

FREE SPEECH, PUBLIC OPINION AND CONSERVATIONISM

Because we are all humans we have more things in common than differences, regardless of the different political aspects and opinions people have. Differences among people seem to exist only in how they interpret the things they have in common with each other. These divergent interpretations can only mean that, in general, there is still a long way to go for people to really understand each other and even themselves. *"We are often as strange to ourselves as we are to other people"*. (Siri Hustvedt)

Going a little further, many of the hate and confrontation people point at in opinions and ideologies they are against, are actually being a way of seeking to affirm their own individuality through others. In this case, it is a way of denying to recognize having in oneself what he or she appoints in those who they seek to differentiate themselves from, who they are against, and at the same times, even when knowing – or feeling an inner discomfort but still unconsciously – that what he or she points at in people they hate is something they fear to have in themselves, they are seeking to reject recognizing it in the self, by repressing it, by projecting this internal fear and bother into the external world, where they can express their discomfort, hate and act against (as a way to protecting the self from self-hate).

Many political movements are surging and gaining attention, advocating against what they call the corruption of the western values, such as Christianity, Patriarchy, Family values, as well as classic and modern thinking and artistic traditions. They call for the right of free speech for feeling they have their voices and opinion repressed by the mainstream politics, by academic institutions and the mainstream media, which they accuse of being dominated with the left wing influence, what they interpret as the imposition of the socialist values in society. For them, it is all part of the new strategy of the left to conquer the western society, by destroying it.

They declare to be rationalists for using facts, logic and science against the passions and irrational left wing desires and alienation, which they believe to be against freedom. They are the Think Tank, performing research and advocacy concerning topics such as social policy, political strategy, economics, military, technology, and culture, with strong ideological-orientation. Most Think Tanks are non-governmental organizations, but some are semi-autonomous agencies within government or are associated with particular political parties, especially millionaires and billionaires, or businesses.

Because they have a strong opposition to the mainstream and center political institutions and parties, academic institutions and social policies, they attract a lot of people who have a strong wish to fight against the status quo, for feeling psychologically and sometimes socially excluded from it.

While they claim to advocate for empiricism and scientific knowledge, according to their discourses, they contradict themselves by being rationalists in practice. They claim to search and support knowledge when in fact they are conservatives advocating for absolutism and certitude. Their strongest campaign is for speech freedom, for the freedom of opinion, when in fact they are extremely radical about eliminating their opponents' opinions.

When people have freedom of opinion they inevitably form different opinions. Only when people have common passion their opinions, if we could call it an opinion, will be the same[1]. The truth of the matter is that no opinion is possible to be formed when all opinions become the same; The so-called public opinion. No one is capable of forming their own opinion without the benefit of the multitude of opinions held by others. The public opinion endangers the individual opinion. On the other hand, the multitude of opinions is the only thing that breaks tyrants and tyrannies. This is why the American found fathers equate public opinion with tyranny, and democracy was to them a new flanged form of nepotism, so they established a Republic instead. It was against democracy that the senators were originally established in classic republics. Their goal was to protect society against the confusion of multitude. While public interest, in politics, belongs to the interest of a group, opinions, on the contrary, never belong to a group but exclusively to individuals. Multitude will never be able to form an opinion[2].

Opinion rises whenever people communicate coolly and freely with one another and have the safety to make their views public. But *"the reason of man, like the man himself, is timid and cautious when left alone, and acquire firmness and confidence when proportion to the number with which it is associated"*[3]. Since opinions are formed and testify during the exchange against others' opinion, their differences can be mediated only through a body of men chosen by this purpose; They are originally the senators, the medium which all public opinion must pass. Without such mediation, to pass opinions through, opinions crystallizes into a variety of conflicting mass sentiments under the pressure of emergency, waiting for a "strong man" to mold them into a unanimous "public opinion", killing all opinions then. Contrary to human reason and opinions, the human power is not only cautious and timid when left alone but completely nonexistent, unless it can rely on others; No King and Tyrants have power without people obeying them. Every support in politics is obedience to a public opinion; and so revolutions.

Demagogues are always talking about freedom, free opinion and free speech against what they accuse to be the tyranny that blocks individual freedom. But their fight demands human power, the support of a multitude that carries a public opinion and never opinions. While they claim to fight for freedom they are mostly likely to be fighting for a tyranny of a strong man or institutions which will guarantee the absolute and imposing permanence of their values, against the threat of free opinions. They claim to support free debate and opinions but they fight against it with eristic dialectics, as an attempt to confuse and tire their opponents, to end any real debate and dialogue, and canceling the political arena.

Their strong absolutist conservatism reflects an internal anxious search and establishment of a safe harbor, that they feel missing in themselves. What they claim to fight against – the socialism, the "postmodernist-marxism", the equality ideology, etc – seems to be a projection of their internal agony against changes in society, for feeling aside from, not belonging to, left behind, looking for something that represents permanence and eternity, which they rationalize to be the later classic and modernist social traditions of patriarchy, republic, capitalist business with their boss culture and so-called democracy.

It is interesting to notice that a huge part of their members are people who feel emotionally isolated, specially men, blaming women and women movements for being against them, associating women to *social chaos against patriarchal tradition*[4], Conservative

Think Tank thinkers rationalize and misinterpret classic works from the matriarchal Greek era and the bible which, contrary to their rationalist interpretations, denounces the human attempt to control nature as the source of chaos. Changes are a natural phenomenon for nature and life symbiosis, and the attempt to stop it for something permanent is what creates chaos. This is why Thomas Jefferson was against a permanent and absolutist constitution and eternal republic. He thought revolutions to be necessary and important for freedom. The permanent and unchangeable constitution was, for him, a tyrannical power prohibiting the future generation to have the freedom of opinion, impeding them to recreate a foundation according to changes they experience in society, just as the American found fathers generation did[5].

The absolutist and eternal establishment of a social order, against what they condemn to create chaos in society, reflects an emotional emptiness which they want to fill. Many of them are men complaining they did not grow up with a father figure, believing it to be the cause of their emotional insecurity towards life, rationalizing the problem as the lack of a patriarchal social order that rips families apart, according to them. It seems that they never learned that most children, from modernity on, grew up without a father figure, even, and specially, during the most conservative patriarchal and family tradition times, because the father had to spend all day outside home in order to work and provide to their families, which was more than just eight working hours and included the weekends. What gave children emotional confidence, instead, was the constant presence and love of the mother at home. Such constant expression of love, through daily affairs and care towards the family and intimate relationships – which does not matter if it comes from the mother, from the father or from foster parents – creates in the child an emotional safe harbor of self confidence, for the unconditional love they received and perceived, which they will carry for the rest of their lives[6]. Without having such safe harbor in themselves, which the person can always return to when they feel uncertain about themselves, the individual becomes insecure for not believing in such unconditional love for themselves. They will feel emotionally indigent, trying to find such safe harbor in others, through their romantic, fraternal and even political relationships, such as in the leader who promise the absolutist social order, of a traditional family and patriarchal traditions, with the hope it will guarantee or give them a better opportunity to find such harbor, where they can hold on and feel safe from the uncertainty of ever changing reality.

Relations are utilitarian but healthy relations are relations with symbiosis, where one works and acts in life for trusting that wherever one sails to one will have a safe harbor in themselves; Because every action is a risk taking in the unpredictability in life. Such confidence and dedication, in their attitude and work in life, generates experiences and skills that form a stronger confidence in their individual acting power, which is reflected in their work and attitude through life as a reliability provider, shaping their personality and identity as an attractive harbor to others. Without such trust in the self what is left is anxiety and frustration, for not being able to develop an attractive harbor through individual action, that forms their self narrative (where identity comes from). In order to protect the self from inner-hate the individual will tend to project such hate to the external world, accusing, then, the external target to be the evil cause of their internal chaos. The external target, where hate is projected, is to be fought and destroyed as symbolism of the destruction of their internal conflicts. Many people, on the other hand, look for professional help but not really looking for understanding and knowledge about themselves. What people look for is certitude. What they want is to fit in a group and the most popular help they will find is focused on it. Not in really improving themselves through understanding but through pretending to belong to a group as their safe harbor. Many of the self-help books and gurus are highly ideologically driven, presenting people with mythology about Patriarchy, Postmodernist, Marxism and all sorts of political excuses to incite hate projection, creating public opinions in support of their ideological agenda.

This is why the family is important, community is important, institutions are important, they are all safe harbor to us, but it doesn't necessarily mean they should never change. They must change to keep up with reality symbiosis that is in constant motion. We are always looking for a safe harbor. When we can not find it in ourselves, in our own world, we will try to find it in the external world, thus attempting to force something that will artificially represent such a harbor. The belief that in introducing a supposed absolutism and permanence we will overcome the insecurity in us. The insecurity of acting in life. The absolutism is to convince the self to have overcome our action unpredictability in a supposed static and pre-visible reality. But such absolutist permanence can only be established through the tyrannical support of public opinion, molded by the power of a strong man; A hero or the father figure, who crystallizes the conflicting mass sentiments under the pressure of emergency, and which the classic Greek hero narratives alert us against[7].

Without realizing it, these conservatives are, before anything else, strongly romantics.

[1] COOKER, J. E. *The Federalist (1787)*. New York: Wesleyan University Press , 1983

[2] ARENDT, H. *On Revolution.* London: Faber & Faber, 2016.

[4] PETERSON. J. *Maps of Meaning: The Architecture of Belief.* Routledge: first edition, 1999

[5] T. JEFFERSON; S. K.I. PADOVER. *The Completly Jefferson*, New York: Distributed by Duell, Sloan & Pearce, Inc. ,1943

[6] WINNICOTT, D.W. *The Child, The Family, and The Outside World.* Cambridge: Perseus Publishing, 1964

[7] RANK, O. *Psychology and The Soul.* Mansfield Center, CT : Martino Publishing, 2011.

Once I had a Brazilian flatmate in Dublin who had just arrived in Ireland. In one of our first conversations he told me about the "prostitutes" in the bohemian neighbourhood called Temple Bar. I was surprised because after couple of years living near Temple Bar I had never seen a sex worker. During the conversation I realized the women he was referring to, as sex workers, were just women wearing mini-skirts – which is a very common women outfit in Ireland and UK, even during winter. For the newcomer from Brazil women showing more legs than he was used to see in public had an automatic association to prostitution.

In my first couple of weeks in Freiburg, Germany, when I was looking for a place to live, I was eating in a bar with my mother when a group of 5 men joined our big table. During the conversation they learned we are Brazilians and told us, with a big enthusiasm, they were going to spend their holidays in Brazil in the following month. After a while I asked one of them, who didn't share the same enthusiasm the others were having, if he was going to spend his holidays in Brazil as well. He answered with a gesture of showing his wedding ring on his finger. I suddenly thought he was suggesting that his friends were going to Brazil with sexual intention, specially because sex tourism in Brazil is very common and many people in Sough Germany have the image of Brazilian women as being easy to take to bed – since Brazilians are often very attracted to foreigners. Maybe I misinterpreted his gesture. Maybe he was just saying that he is not as free to travel as his friends who are single, because of family responsibilities, but I could not help thinking about sex tourism through his silent message.

I think it is interesting the fact that among Brazil, Ireland and Germany the first is the more conservative and moralist when the subject is nudity, which is a false morality to protect them from their own dirty minds. Different from Germany, with many parks and saunas where people can spend their time – on their own, with friends or with their families – completely naked. During summer in Germany toddlers are running and playing completely naked in their gardens, while in Brazil parents are concerned about their toddlers private parts or concerned about their toddlers underwear being exposed in public. In Brazil there are some isolated beaches with nude areas but in general nudity is not tolerated or allowed – not even topless regarding women. Nudity in Brazil is automatically associated with sexual provocation. Ireland and the UK do not have the open air or nude sauna culture as in the Nordic countries but nobody minds women showing their skin. Once a naked woman walking in the streets in the UK was stopped by a policeman, not to reprimand her but to inform her about the law, saying that her being nude in public is not an offense but if somebody complains for feeling offended then it becomes an offense.

Any bath place is supposed to be a place where people do not need to wear clothes. In South France, where it used to be common for people to be nude in beaches, people, and specially women, feel less comfortable with nudity because of the new generation of young men who automatically associate naked women as a sign of *available for sex*. Women, thus, became more frequent victims of harassment.

When I started with photography, in Ireland, it was always easy to find people to photograph, especially women. Soon I had my first boudoir photo shoot which for my surprise ended as nude photo shoot. It was a woman who contacted me, looking for sensual photos but during the photo shoot she felt comfortable enough to just take out her clothes and continuous the shooting naked. Thanks to her I had photos for my portfolio which brought me more women wanting nude photos, especially after I developed a classic visual language with film negative photos that people became attracted to. Most people associate nude photography with pornography – anything can be turned into pornography in fact, it only requires the viewer imagination and intention[1] – but it is not how I see my work. As a man I am naturally interested in women's beauty and women's body but it doesn't mean I have the sexual view about people I photograph for them being naked; I have a big respect for people who trust me and my work, since most of my photo shoots are just me and the model.

Some people, especially in Brazil, quickly ask me if I sleep with the models I photograph, because they can not help associating nudity to sexual activity. Nudity, instead, gives people a sense of freedom. I only photographed a couple of nude men and it was more evident from them their enthusiasm for being naked in front of the camera – and for having a creative image of their body expression. I first noticed it when I was photographing a woman who the body seemed stucked during my posing direction. I told her that she does not look comfortable and that I could not get good body composition from her. She then asked me if I could see her private parts, to which I replied saying that I am too concentrated on the body composition, lighting, camera setting, framing, lens focusing and on the image narrative, that looking at her private parts never crossed my mind. It seemed to me her worries came from the fact I was photographing her with an old manual film camera with a slow focus ring in the lens; Because of the system it takes me a little extra time to find the lens focus before I press the camera shutter release, causing her to wonder if I was creeping her private parts through the camera viewfinder. I tried to explain about the camera to her but she was satisfied with my first explanation; She did not want to hear about my camera but go on with the photo shoot, this time feeling completely free with no worries about what in her body may be exposed, even if it appears in the photo. It is through people's eyes where we confirm who we are[2].

We fear people's judgment which makes us feel self-conscious. When we are self-conscious we feel uncomfortable, feeling uneasy and dissociated from the place and people around us, alien to our surroundings, causing us to cover who we are – looking for the *self*'s privacy. Being naked and being accepted as we are without clothes means self-confirmation, and so self-acceptance. It gives people more confidence about their body and so about themselves, because they can do whatever they are doing and forget about themselves, feeling more connected to whatever they are doing and their bodies, enjoying the moment completely and so feeling free. Many people ask me how I convince people to take their clothes off or how I convince women to have certain poses when naked. I never needed to convince anybody to do anything, it was all their decision in the first place, for their self-disclosure, to the joy of appearing in the world and deed without equivocation and without self-reflection that are inherent in action[3].

In Germany it is much more difficult to have people who want nude photo shoots. Instead of paying me they want to be paid. Often it has to do with the fact that Germans are more cynic, for feeling suspicious about people's intentions, especially those who they don't know in person. German introversion makes them feel more alienated from people and so more self-conscious, which explains the awkwardness that often Germans have. But this cynicism and uneasy feeling among strangers is not the main reason, it seems. I believe the main reason is because they are more used and comfortable enough with their naked body in public. Instead of photo shoots, for the creative expression of their body freedom, they rather go to saunas and nude public parks where they can enjoy the freedom of their bodies without the need of interaction with another person, but on their own, or with their family, in their introverted manner.

The ancient Greek had the Polis, the public space where people could interact and become equal to others, which separate them from their private life where people had their own individuality. This public space was, for Theseus, what enabled ordinary man to bear life's burden, for providing the safe space for public interaction. But it was also where people hide their individuality in order to become equals and so respect each other[4]. The medieval Christianity thinking and social tradition had no Polis separating the public and the private. People became equal to each other not through a political space designated for political interaction but through every individual where God becomes ubiquitous in every person's eyes, turning people's presence into an establishment of the public space and their action towards people as action towards God itself.[5] Consequently, people had to hide more of themselves in order to preserve their individuality and privacy. I feel Germans keep something of this separation of public and private tradition, with their closed friend circle as their Polis, where they can interact and express themselves to each other as equal while outside it they can be "naked", with no need to hide their individuality in order to preserve it; Or as Germans like to say, *"being direct"*. The Irish, maintaining a more medieval Christian tradition, have the public space on every person's eyes, who they can interact and express themselves with in order to bear life's burden together, but hiding their individuality in order to preserve it. The photo shooting seems to be the private sphere for the Irish, where people can be free from the public "burden" but, at the same time, they can appear to the public by showing their individual expression, through photo results; since it is only through others' eyes we can confirm ourselves, including our private *self*. It also seems to be the reason the so-called "German directness" is interpreted as rudeness by Anglican and Latin cultures. Politeness is in fact against directness; Hiding our true thinking and wishes to act, our individuality, to respect those through whom we see ourselves as in the eyes of the public arena – God ubiquitous. Germans feel free to not hide much of their true feelings because what the Irish see as public is for the German seen as private; the private space where people can have their individuality and action without the public "burden". The German introversion seems to be a preservation of their individuality in a private sphere, which for the Irish is supposed to be public.

In today's society there is no such thing as private space other than our own home[6]. The patriarchal family was supposed to be the private kingship where one can have its individuality freedom apart from the public burden – The reason the Greeks, originally a matriarchal society, created the Polis, as contrast to the private patriarchal little kingdom[7]. God ubiquitous came to replace the Polis during Medieval times. The equality ideology we have today is what replaced God ubiquitous from medieval societies. Universal equality invades even the patriarchal family – the private kingdom – in order to assure people's basic equality rights.

Different cultures find their way to appear and to hide. In order to keep prolific with nude photography, after moving to Germany, I started photographing myself; this time with pinhole cameras that work with long exposure photographs. I never felt completely comfortable being nude in public – especially coming from a judging and mocking culture that is strong in Brazil; Where the public and the private are merged and confused because of the attempt to find their individual expression in public and, at the same time, afraid of losing both all together – but doing my creative work, that now includes my own body expression, made me feel very good and more comfortable in my own body. Like a work of art we create from our own expression the body becomes a work of art – it has always been in fact – through which we find our individuality in our nudity and, at the same time, our public expression through the image result. The public where we confirm our own self narrative, which without we have no identity.

[1] HUSTVEDT, S. A Plea for Eros. Separata de; HUSTVEDT, S. *A Plea for Eros: Essays.* NY: Picador, 2006

[2] ARENDT, H. *The Life of the Mind: The groundbreaking investigation on how we think.* New York: Houghton Mifflin Harcourt, 1977.

[3,4,5] ARENDT, H. *On Revolution.* London: Faber & Faber, 2016.

[6] ARENDT, H. *The Human Condition*: Chicago: University of Chicago Press, 2018. Second Edition.

[7] RANK, O. *Psychology and The Soul.* Mansfield Center, CT : Martino Publishing, 2011.

ABOUT WRITING AND WOUNDS

I am far from being a greater writer. I have no writing skills to show of; I write because I have to. I used to have a blog where I published my poetry when I was in my earlier 20's and sometimes I had extensive prose writings but it is only nowadays I feel more comfortable about writing; I care less about how people will judge me through what they read from me and much less about what may be their judgment about my poor writing style, wrong grammar and misspellings. Being away from the environment where I grew up, where I felt constantly judged, gave me more sense of freedom. I embrace whatever wrong I do as part of me, so as part of what I do, instead of repressing myself. It does not mean I do not try to improve; It means that in order to improve I have to accept first who I am. My main goal is not improvement although I hope it will come on its own time through practice and eventual help from kind people, if it comes. I can not really tell what my goal is, I just have to make concrete what I have as feelings and impressions, through my work. *Our wholeness and continuity are not given but made in us by ourselves*, with the materialization of our memories through stories, where memories become permanent.

I used to feel writing was a challenge, a dangerous things, because it is where people can literally reads and judge the author, and I was judged enough at school for being not good in my studies, judged in my neighborhood for being considered slow mind with my distraction, and even mocked among my family members not only because of Brazilian judging and mocking culture but also because of my own family members immaturity. I never felt I was understood through what I do, feeling a strong pressure and demand from people, of having to explain myself about what I could not even explain, explanation about why I do things the way I do and think the way I think. Such demands for justifications only caused me anxieties. My individuality disturbed the strong Brazilian demands for differentiation allowed only through skills and ready made concepts I never had. I found my individuality being safer expressed through other means such as drawing, paining and later on through photography.

Drawing and paintings were to compensate for my writing insecurities. Later it was photography compensating for my drawings and paintings insecurities – also because of practical impediments – and today I feel writing is back again, coming to compensate for what I miss in photography. Insecurities are not my only issue but circumstances, which I believe to be what affects the most my insecurities.

In her essay called **Leaving Your Mother** Siri Hustvedt wrote that *a child's true independence is the product of a strong, reassuring parental presence, and it is that presence that we take with us when we walk out the door for good.* I feel the lack of such reassuring presence hunts me. My confidence emerges only in isolation or through people who provide their reassuring presence to me. The reassuring presence is before anything else the trust on what I do without any need of explanation and regardless of my imperfection, which gives me the confidence that I will not disappoint even if I fail. It is the solid ground which we call home, where we always go back whenever feeling apart, judged and not trusted for not being understood; The place where we find unconditional love.

For not feeling judged and with no need to explain myself I feel understood, and from understanding I feel accepted without having to communicate anything as justification. This is true for every individual and such foundation is what has to be built during infancy for the individual to become an independent adult. Once the assuring parental presence leaves, the child feels guilty believing their aggressive manners and cries in frustration are the causes of their parental or caretaker detachment. Such belief makes the child hate themselves and, then, transfer such hate to their caretaker or parents, growing without a ground which they can believe they are accepted, welcomed, trusted and loved no matter what, fearing they can disappoint people at any moment. To overcome it, people find their ways to compensate for their insecurities, which can be many according to each individual and how wounded they feel, even if they never perceive it consciously.

Being able to focus our mind on something and become unaware of our own *self* is the experience's characteristic of many artists, which is often experienced in isolation. It is as if embracing who they are, as being apart from the social dominant psychology, and through such isolation is where they find their own ground in their own creative work. It seems to be the reason many artists are willing to challenge and risk everything for their artistic passion; it is not a simple romanticism idealism, it is all they have as ground for their *self*. Most artists will not succeed in having both an individual and social world which they can live in and find their individual and social achievements, they live, instead, in an eternal conflict between both worlds. Especially in poverty where artists often find they have to give up their individual world, in order to keep the jobs they need, and so a roof above their heads and food on the table. Not only that but also the conflict between isolation and the *social capital,* that is fundamental for success in society;

Many artists will find their people, the ones they recognize themselves with and where they find their ground with, in the bohemian artist groups, in art school or universities. But some people will never find it. People come and go. They do not want to be in the academy and they feel it may be a threat to their own independent minds and personalities.

I always felt it but it was never as clear to me; how I have been looking for a place where I can be isolated and, yet, still be able to step in social interaction where we find the confirmation about who we are. My thought was that I was running, escaping, in order to be free. Such thinking turns up to be true; the escaping from my own insecurities, hunting for my own ground. While I was told I am brave for traveling to a foreigner country on my own with only $1000 in 2008, I never felt it to be any act of bravery but a desperate escape. It was the best experience I had, the feeling of freedom and novelty, a confidence I have never had before to finally find myself on my own. If *only the unprotected self can feel joy,* my confidence on leaving home came from the ground I found in my creative act in my own isolation, where I could confirm my own self through my individual act. Today I find such confidence to be shaken by a lack of a place where I can isolate myself and act.

In **Extracts From A Story of The Wounded Self**, Siri Hustvedt tells her isolating experiences in libraries at her hometown, in Norway through their night readings, and in New York at her apartment while living in poverty, where through thin walls she could hear all kinds of noises from her neighbours. While she was able to use her typewriter and read in such living conditions, I find it impossible for me to do the same in a similar situation I live in today. She could find her isolation where I can not. I speculate it has something to do with the fact that she found her people through university, which is also where she found her love; Paul

Auster. They found each other and created their own ground without the fear of disappointing each other, without running from what they had because they felt security in themselves, a home where they could return. The same as I felt when traveling to Israel, which despite all troubles I succeeded in arriving in my final destination, a Kibbutz. I was not scared or worried. My thought was that whatever happened I could always just return to my isolation back home, in Brazil.

> "I held fiercely to the lonely idea of my own great
> destiny, and I suspect that I clung to this irrational
> position for a single reason: my parents loved me very
> well. It was plain that my mother and my father
> thought I was wonderful. They made me feel that
> nothing was beyond me, and their belief in me and in
> my three younger sisters was unshakable, as a fortress
> into which we could retreat whenever we needed it.
> [...]. We are, all of us, made from our parents,
> physically and emotionally, and the quality we call
> "character" partakes of both genetic and the
> mysterious meanderings of a particular psychic
> history" (Siri Hustvetd, 2004)

In Israel I felt envious of a girl who used to write in her journal. To me it was an act of bravery. She was clearly a wounded girl but still confident enough in herself to write, fearing nothing for finding her ground in it. Just as Paul Auster impressed me with his book **Winter Journal**, where he writes openly about his experiences without worries of people's judgment, without fear of disappointments. Only a person with a place called home can be that brave. It is only possible through the belief of an unconditional love for the self; the home where one can return and retreat the self when needed. I never dared read any other works from Auster. I love how he writes and his bravery but I feel scared of not finding the same in his other works, and so losing the confidence he gives to me. I didn't know Siri Hustvedt, his wife, when I read his book. I only realized they were married when I read about the same car accident story from Siri Hustvedt's book **A Woman Looking at Men Looking at Women**, and I never dared reading any other book from her that are not essays. Such fear of losing something in me that I found in others gives me a great anxiety and a sense of urgency. The greater act of bravery of these two I find to be in their encounter without running from each other, without fearing disappointment and losing, without fearing further wounds. Opposing to what I feel that makes me step away from people and relationships, for not believing in unconditional love for myself.

Reading is where I find the pleasure of novelty, like traveling and arts. Also surprises and emotions I feel through people's stories, through which I can forget my own *self* and live others' life experiences. Siri Hustvedt is great at providing me that, especially when I feel hopeless in my single room apartment with thin walls, in insistent sniffing sounds in German libraries and their oblivious manner. Places where many people would find their isolation but I always feel disturbed with the insistent presence of people around me, with my attention alerted in expectation of the next distracting noise.

After more than four weeks without being able to have enough sleep, reading, writing and photographing I finally found myself in rare summer silence again. I hoped to use this silence to find comfort in the reading of a last essay, **Extracts From A Story of The Wounded Self**, before finally finishing a Siri Hustvedt's book. Instead of comfort, it ended up giving me fears, the confirmation that I will never find my people but in books, and I will never find myself but in isolation, which I can't find today and may never find again.

> "But the worst was that as time wore on, I became
> more and more afraid of myself, or perhaps more and
> more conscious of the fear I have always had – a fear
> that within me is some danger I can't name." (**Siri
> Hustvetd**, 2004)

For Otto Rank, the hero is the artist type, the one who differentiates themselves and goes beyond. But it is precisely in their great act asserting their differentiation, and so find themselves in a ground of their own, that lays the tragedy, for they never had where to belong in the first place. *Is the writing self an answer to the wounded self?* Asks Siri Hustvedt. *Where does the need for writing come from? What is it? It is a need, not a choice. It is a giving away and a giving up.* The only hope in finding my ground in my isolated individual act.